THE CAMBRIDGE UNIVERSITY PRESS FILM HANDBOOKS SERIES

General Editor

Andrew Horton, *University of Oklahoma*

Each CAMBRIDGE FILM HANDBOOK is intended to focus on a single film from a variety of theoretical, critical, and contextual perspectives. This "prism" approach is designed to give students and general readers valuable background and insight into the cinematic, artistic, cultural, and sociopolitical importance of individual films by including chapters by leading film scholars and critics. Furthermore, these handbooks by their very nature are meant to help the reader better grasp the nature of the critical and theoretical discourse on cinema as an art form, as a visual medium, and as a cultural product. Filmographies and select bibliographies are included to help the reader go further on his or her own exploration of the film under consideration.

Francis Ford Coppola's *Godfather Trilogy*

Edited by

NICK BROWNE

CAMBRIDGE
UNIVERSITY PRESS

PUBLISHED BY THE PRESS SYNDICATE OF THE UNIVERSITY OF CAMBRIDGE
The Pitt Building, Trumpington Street, Cambridge, United Kingdom

CAMBRIDGE UNIVERSITY PRESS
The Edinburgh Building, Cambridge CB2 2RU, UK   http://www.cup.cam.ac.uk
40 West 20th Street, New York, NY 10011-4211, USA   http://www.cup.org
10 Stamford Road, Oakleigh, Melbourne 3166, Australia
Ruiz de Alarcón 13, 28014 Madrid, Spain

© Cambridge University Press 2000

First published 2000

Printed in the United States of America

Typeface Stone Serif 9.75/14 pt.   *System* QuarkXPress® [GH]

A catalog record for this book is available from the British Library.

Library of Congress Cataloging-in-Publication Data

Francis Ford Coppola's Godfather trilogy / edited by Nick Browne
    p.   cm. – (Cambridge film handbooks)
    Filmography: p.
    Includes bibliographical references and index.
    ISBN 0-521-55084-X (hardcover)
    1. Godfather films – History and criticism. I. Browne, Nick.
II. Series. Cambridge film handbooks series.
    PN1997.C56833F73   1999
    791.43'75 – dc21   99-17674
                                                          CIP

ISBN 0 521 55084 X hardback
ISBN 0 521 55950 2 paperback

For Mona and Sabrina

Contents

Acknowledgments   *page* xi

List of Contributors   xiii

Fearful A-Symmetries
Violence as History in the *Godfather* Films
NICK BROWNE   1

I **If History Has Taught Us Anything . . . Francis Coppola,**
Paramount Studios, and *The Godfather Parts I, II, and III*
JON LEWIS   23

2 ***The Godfather* and the Mythology of Mafia**
ALESSANDRO CAMON   57

3 **The Representation of Ethnicity in *The Godfather***
VERA DIKA   76

4 **Ideology and Genre in the *Godfather* Films**
GLENN MAN   109

5 **Family Ceremonies: or, Opera in *The Godfather* Trilogy**
NAOMI GREENE   133

Filmography   157

Reviews of the "Godfather" Trilogy   167

Select Bibliography   183

Index   185

Acknowledgments

With appreciation to Dr. Jess Kraus, Director of the Southern California Injury Prevention Research Center, UCLA School of Public Health, for continuing advice and support and to the students in the seminars in the UCLA Department of Film and Television on "Violence in American Film" for continous insight into this topic.

Contributors

Nick Browne is Professor of Film Studies at UCLA. He is the author of *The Rhetoric of Film Narration* (UMI Press, 1982) and *The History of Western Film Theory* (Beijing: China Film Press, 1994) and has edited *The Politics of Representation: Perspectives from Cahiers du Cinéma* (Harvard University Press, 1990), *American Television: New Directions in History and Theory* (1994), *New Chinese Cinemas: Forms, Identities, Politics* (Cambridge University Press, 1994), and *American Film Genres: History and Theory* (University of California Press, 1998). He is presently engaged in a study of violence in contemporary American film.

Alessandro Camon is Vice-President of Production of Edward R. Pressman Film Corporation, the producer of such films as *Badlands, Conan the Barbarian, Wall Street, Reversal of Fortune, Bad Lieutenant*, and *The Crow*. Camon took his degree in philosophy at the University of Padova in 1987 and studied film at UCLA as a Fulbright Scholar. He has been a programming executive for a major Italian TV network and entertainment columnist for an Italian newspaper. He is the author of several Italian language books on American cinema, notably *Il Killer dentro di noi: crimine e violenza nel cinema americano* (*The Killer Inside Us: Crime and Violence in American Cinema*, 1987).

Vera Dika holds a Ph.D. in Cinema Studies from New York University and teaches American cinema at both UCLA and the University of Southern California. She wrote *Games of Terror*, a study of the contemporary American horror film (Fairleigh Dickinson University Press, 1991), and published film criticism for *The LA Times, Art in America*, and *Artforum*.

Naomi Greene is Professor in the Department of French and Italian and is a faculty member in the Film Studies Program at the University of California at Santa Barbara. She has published books on Artaud, René Clair, and most recently on Pier Palo Pasolini (Princeton University Press, 1990) and is currently embarking on a study of the relations between opera and film.

Jon Lewis is Professor in the Department of English at Oregon State University. He has published widely in film and cultural studies. His first book, *The Road to Romance and Ruin: Teen Films and Youth Culture* (Routledge, 1992), received an Outstanding Academic Book Award from *Choice*. His second book, *Whom God Wishes to Destroy: Francis Coppola and the New Hollywood*, was published by Duke University Press in 1995.

Glenn Man is Professor and Chair of the English Department at the University of Hawaii at Manoa. His articles on film have appeared in the *New Orleans Review, Film Criticism, Literature/Film Quarterly*, and *East-West Film Journal*. His study of American film, *Radical Visions: American Film Renaissance, 1967–1976* (Greenwood Press), was published in 1994.

Francis Ford Coppola's *Godfather* Trilogy

Francis Ford Coppola, the director. Copyright Paramount Pictures, 1972. Courtesy of the Museum of Modern Art Film Stills Archive

NICK BROWNE

Fearful A-Symmetries

VIOLENCE AS HISTORY IN THE
GODFATHER FILMS

By almost any account, the *Godfather* films are monu-
ments on the landscape of American cinema. There are, of course,
differences of intention and achievement among the three, but
the first one, *The Godfather* (1972), stands out in popular and critical opinion as one of the enduring works of the American cinema.
The standing of *The Godfather Part II* (1974), nearly comparable to
the first, lies not only in its art, but in its outlook, so rare in American films from early 1970s, on a flawed American protagonist as
an emblem of American empire. *The Godfather Part III* brings out
the theme of redemption present in Coppola's vision from the
start. It is natural to regard these films as a trilogy to deal with the
continuity of a directorial vision of the century-long working
through of economic crime and punishment in the inner sanctum
of an American dynasty.

As a commercial venture, *The Godfather* and, to a lesser extent,
The Godfather Part II were blockbusters. In its day, *The Godfather*
was one of the most profitable films of all time. Over the years, it
is said, the trilogy did business of more than a billion dollars. *The
Godfather* continues to be loved by the public and remains one of
the few enduring, still popular classics of American cinema. The
films were breakout, critical successes as well, earning more than
two dozen Academy Award nominations among them. *The Godfather* (1972) and *The Godfather Part II* (1974) both won Academy
Awards as "Best Picture." Coppola and Puzo won twice for "Best

Adapted Screenplay." Coppola won "Best Director" for *II*. Brando
and DeNiro both won acting awards. Moreover, the first two films
amounted to a social phenomenon – they entered into every level
of American culture – high and low – sometimes by attitude,
sometimes by quotation, and sometimes through their iconic, signature scenes. The first two films entered not only movie history,
but American mythology as well, and have stayed there for more
than twenty-five years.

The distinctiveness of the *Godfather* trilogy lies at the intersec-
tion of the national character of the system of American film genres and the tradition of the European art cinema. These works
exhibit a very high level of craft in the making of the film. The
sets, costumes, lighting, cinematography, sound, music, editing,
and so on together provide an extraordinary level of sensuous
delight in cinematic design and presentation. The *Godfather* films
are, moreover, deeply rooted in the conventions of the American
crime film and the social experience of the ambitious outsider that
shapes that genre's attitudes. The distinctiveness of Coppola's and
Puzo's adaptation of Puzo's novel lies in its reinterpretation of the
generic conventions of the crime film in the direction of the family melodrama and the epic. It is this transformation of subject
matter that gives the films their popular appeal.

The Coppola aesthetic, that is to say the sensibility and concept
that informs these works, is at the same time realist and theatrical.
The films might even be regarded as antimodernist in the way
they foreground action taking place in the photographed world
without the need for special effects and in the understated transparency of their cinematic technique. Notwithstanding the fact
that some of the most celebrated scenes are those assembled by
Eisenstein-like juxtaposition (for example, the intercutting of the
execution of the enemies with Michael's godson's baptism that
includes the line "Do you renounce Satan?"), the Coppola aesthetic is ultimately one of "mise-en-scène" – that is to say of acting, blocking, and delivery of dialog. The narrative of *The Godfather* possesses the simplicity of linear development by plausible

complication following reliable dramatic laws of action and reaction. *Godfather II*'s narrative architecture – the alternation of present and past – taking the viewer back through the century – though initially complicating – locates the contemporary story of the 1950s and 1960s squarely within a chronological presentation of American history. This history takes the form of repetition with a difference – namely, underlining the progressive loss of aura and the weakening justification for violence through a narrative pattern of parallelism and counterpoint – for example, the comparison of opening festivals, the decisive act of murder that launches and establishes both godfathers, and so on.

The films' power is closely connected to the tour-de-force performances of Brando and especially Pacino and to the distinctively American style of acting – "the method" – that they embody. The brilliance of Coppola's direction per se (that is, beyond the forcefulness and ingenuity needed to write and cast the films) consists of two parts. The first is eliciting from actors, individually and together, performances that convincingly take the character across the changes of time and experience to render absolutely definitive crystalizations of Coppola's interpretation of the story as the decline of honor in the ascent to power. He shapes Brando's aging, judicious, distracted benevolence with the emergence of Pacino's movement away from simple filial duty toward the calculating, aggressive, repressed, and hypocritical killer of foe and family that he becomes. The second quality of Coppola's direction consists of the discovery of a cinematic style, principally through framing and composition of individual shots, that gives epic force and meaning to the actors' work. It is a cinema of transparency, a cinematic style that has no need to call attention to itself but only to display the inherent theatricality of the action taking place in the middle distance, for it is the framelines and the lighting that create dark hollows and zones of significant illumination that give meaning to the actors' looks, movement, and lines. This cinematic style does not present but discloses the drama. The dialogue is not literary though it comes from a novel, but seems to issue directly from the milieu. The opening shot of *The Godfather* is a striking anomaly to the norm that confirms this thesis. Beginning with a riveting story of insult and injustice recounted by the undertaker Bonasera directly to the camera, the drama unfolds by an almost imperceptible slow reverse zoom that moves across the desk to disclose a listener and stops behind the shoulder of the unidentified figure – the Godfather – as we see in the reverse shot. This technique, possible perhaps only in cinema, clearly defines the space of the actor, aligns it to the principal character, and underlines the inherently spatial integrity of the drama. It is this concept of a stable, centered space and the determined positions of the actors in the frame that helps to give the characters their particular dramatic and epic weight. The cinematic frames, though deliberately composed, are rarely beautiful in their own right, but function both to recount the story and to interpret it by tone, scale, and texture. Rarely has American cinema made such powerful use of overtones to dramatize a scene. The importance of *Godfather* films lies both in their knowledge and redeployment of the conventions of the genre and in a directoral intelligence operating within the most distinctive traditions of American theater as adapted to cinema.

The writing on the *Godfather* films has mostly been journalistic. Apart from a few articles in small journals, writers of articles and books usually have documented the production of the films – that is to say, the hiring of Coppola; the writing, the casting, and the shooting; the history of troubles on the set; the story of the Mafia, and so forth. The result has been a comprehensive picture of the inner workings of the production of the movies. Coppola, by contrast, has offered expansive and frank statements about his aesthetic ambitions and the intentions that informed the films. What is often missing from the general critical picture of these films is analysis of the form, function, and significance of the films and the social and artistic context of Coppola's achievement. This book provides an orientation to these critical topics for persons who want to go beyond production history, personality, and anecdote to view these works critically as American masterpieces.

Marlon Brando, the Godfather. *The Godfather* (1972), Copyright Paramount Pictures, 1972. Courtesy of the Museum of Modern Art Film Stills Archive

SYNOPSIS

The Godfather (1972) is the story of the struggle of the Corleone family of New York, principally its head Don Vito and his youngest son Michael, to maintain and eventually transform the family business in the face of murderous challenges by other Mafia families to their preeminent position. Ultimately, it is the story of father and sons, and of an old world and the new, and of Michael's succession to power as head of the family.

The film opens at the family compound on Long Island in 1945 with the grand wedding of the Don's daughter Connie and with Michael's return from the war accompanied by his fiancée, Kay. From within his darkened sanctuary/office, the Don dispenses justice to an aggrieved petitioner and agrees to help his godson get a leading part in an upcoming Hollywood movie.

The film's story moves decisively forward with "the Turk's" (Sollozzo's) request for the Don's help – a million-dollar loan and access to the Corleones' political network of judges, politicians, and police – in order to expand his criminal empire in narcotics. When the Don refuses in order not to jeopardize his other businesses, Sollozzo's partners kill Luca Brasi, the Corleones' number one tough guy, shoot the Don himself, leaving him wounded in the street, and kidnap the Don's number one adviser, his adopted son Tom, a lawyer who he expects will negotiate a peace. Fredo, the second son, is left crying in the street. With the Don in the hospital, the eldest son, the hot-blooded Sonny, plans an all-out frontal attack against Sollozzo's associates. On a visit to the hospital, Michael discovers and foils a second attempt on his father's life. Seeing that his wounded father will remain in danger until a decisive step is taken to eliminate the threat, he coolly plans and carries out a daring execution of Sollozzo and his police ally McCluskey by shooting them point blank in a quiet restaurant. Michael secretes himself in Sicily under the protection of his father's old friend.

The war between the families expands. Sonny is set up by Connie's husband Carlo and Michael is set up by his own bodyguard. Sonny is killed, but a bomb intended for Michael explodes, killing his young Sicilian wife instead. To end the killing and bring Michael home, Don Vito negotiates a peace by making a political accommodation with the other families – Barzini and Tattaglia. Michael returns as head of the Corleone family and as time passes convinces Kay to marry him – promising that the business is soon to be fully legitimate. He plans to resettle the family and its business in Las Vegas by taking over the casino in one of the big hotels run by Moe Greene.

The rival families in New York, however, plan to have Michael killed. Drawing on his long experience of interfamily war, the Don tells Michael that he will be betrayed by someone in his own group. After expressing regret for the life Michael has entered and the lost opportunities of possible legitimate power, the Don dies quietly while playing with his grandson. The funeral shows who the traitor is, and Michael plans his revenge for Sonny's murder. While Michael stands godfather to his nephew's baptism, his enemies from within his own group – Tessio, and Connie's husband, Carlo – and the others from without – the heads and operatives of the rival families (Barzini, Tattaglia, Cuneo, and Stracchi and Moe Greene) – are slaughtered one by one. When confronted by his wife Kay with responsibility for Carlo's death, Michael denies it. The film ends as Michael closes the door against his wife and his lieutenants bow to kiss his hand, recognizing Michael officially as the new Godfather.

The Godfather Part II (1974) interweaves two related stories – that of the coming of age of Vito Corleone (the aging Don of the first film) in the early part of the century (1901–1918) and the struggles of his son Michael in his conduct and defense of Mafia business in Las Vegas, Havana, and Washington, DC, in the late 1950s. The film tells a story of the corruptions of power and personal price that Michael must pay for its exercise.

These two historically distinct stories are presented in alternating strands beginning in 1901 with the murder of Vito's father by a Sicilian Mafia Don and his escape to America, and concludes with Michael alone outside his mansion at Lake Tahoe in Nevada. Vito's story, set in Little Italy, concerns his friendship with the young Clemenza, and the beginning of his life of crime, culminating in the murder of the local Black Hand boss and his elevation to a man deserving respect.

Don Michael's story, the present of the film, begins at a party in Lake Tahoe celebrating his son Anthony's first communion. Michael and a U.S. senator from Nevada discuss the arrangements for a gambling license for a Las Vegas hotel. Michael rejects the senator's demand for a payoff and turns instead to consider a possible partnership with Hyman Roth, a Florida Mafia chief and old friend of his father. Frankie Pentangeli, now head of the Corleones' businesses in New York, asks Michael's help in eliminating the Rosato brothers' challenge to his control. But Roth is the patron of the Rossatos and Michael declines.

After an attempt on his life, Michael leaves his business in Nevada to Tom and joins in a partnership with Roth. Shortly after, Senator Geary falls under Corleone control when he is found with a dead prostitute. In New York the Rossatos, with the secret help of Fredo, Michael's weak brother, bungle an attempt on Pentangeli's life.

Michael joins Roth in a provisional agreement with the Cuban dictator in Havana to take over gambling there. Against the backdrop of a popular revolution that unseats the dictator, Michael decides to pull out and discovers that his brother Fredo has been secretly assisting Hyman Roth and was in fact involved in the attempt at Lake Tahoe on his life. Michael confronts a guilty Fredo, who flees. Before departing a chaotic Havana, Michael tries unsuccessfully to have Roth killed. He returns home to learn that his wife has miscarried.

Pentangeli, believing that Michael tried to have him killed, turns state's evidence. Michael is called before a Senate committee investigating organized crime, but with Senator Geary's public defense of his good character and Pentangeli's curious refusal to testify, the inquiry collapses. Kay tells Michael she intends to leave him and that contrary to what he was led to believe, she had an abortion – refusing to bring another Corleone son into the world and declaring "all this must end." Michael and Kay become completely estranged.

At the funeral of their mother, Connie asks Michael's forgiveness for her neglect and for her brother Fredo. Michael plans his final revenge for the attack on him and his family. Pentangeli commits suicide like a good soldier and Michael arranges to have Roth and finally his brother Fredo killed. A flashback shows a young idealistic Michael who has just enlisted in the Marines at a festive birthday party in 1941 with his father and brothers. The final scene shows Michael after having seen his brother killed sitting alone and bereft against a cold winter sky.

The Godfather Part III (1990) opens eight years after *Part II* ended with a desolate and now derelict mansion at Lake Tahoe. Don Michael Corleone has moved to New York City, is divorced from Kay who has since remarried, and is separated from his children. The haunting memory of the death of his brother Fredo remains on his mind.

The story proper begins on the day Michael – now fully legitimate – is to be recognized by the Pope for his philanthropic work by his induction into the distinguished Order of Saint Sebastian. At the festive celebration afterward, he meets his grown-up son Anthony who declares that he refuses to participate in family business and will pursue a singing career instead. His daughter Mary meets and falls for her cousin Vincent Mancini, Sonny Corleone's hot-blooded, grown-up illegitimate child. The inheritor of the Corleone business interests in New York is now Joey Zaza. Michael is asked to arbitrate the bad blood between Zaza and Vincent, his lieutenant. Each wants the other dead. Vincent declares he wants to protect Michael, and Michael slowly agrees to introduce Vincent into the ways of the world.

The archbishop in charge of the Vatican Bank asks Michael for financial assistance. The bank, it turns out, has lost more than $700 million. Michael, seeking a way to wash away his history in crime, agrees to deposit $600 million when he is recognized as chairman of a venerable European holding company, Immobiliare, in which the Church has a 25 percent stake. The archbishop agrees pending final ratification by the Pope in Rome. The other Mafia families of New York want, of course, to be part of the deal, but Michael refuses and terminates his business relationship with them by giving each, except Zaza, a generous payout. Zaza, insulted, declares war. The meeting ends with a helicopter attack, killing many of the heads of the families and leaving the question: Who is behind Zaza – who is the secret enemy? Though Michael's $600 million has been deposited with the bank, ratification of his appointment as chairman is delayed when the Pope falls ill.

Michael has a diabetic stroke and has to be removed to the hospital. While Michael is recovering, Mary and Vincent consummate their romance, and with Connie's okay, Vincent kills Zaza. Upon recovering, Michael sets up with his old friend in Sicily, Don Tomassino, in order to celebrate Anthony's debut at the Palermo Opera House. Lucchesi, a high official in the Vatican banking hierarchy, is identified as the probable prime mover behind Zaza. Michael begins to distrust Altabello, and the go-between, and through Vincent intrigues to bring out Altabello's true colors. He learns that Altabello and Lucchesi are plotting his murder. Michael is introduced to a good priest, Father Lamberto. He confides his financial problem and for the first time in his adult life, makes a confession including the fact that he ordered his brother's death. Michael asks Kay as well for forgiveness.

The plot to cover up financial fraud at the Vatican and the plot to kill Michael proceed. The ill Pope dies and the good priest is elected to replace him. Michael, sick and seeking redemption, turns over the management of the counterplot and his protection to Vincent. Vincent is recognized by Michael as the new Don Corleone, but there is a price. Vincent must renounce his love for Mary and definitively separate from her. The new Pope sets out to clean up Vatican finances and ratifies the Immobliare deal, effectively installing Michael as chairman. While the premiere of *Cavalleria Rusticana,* an opera of betrayal and revenge, unfolds in Palermo, Michael's counterplot unfolds in Rome through his agents: Altabello is poisoned at the opera, the deceitful archbishop is shot, Lucchesi is stabbed, and Keinszig ("God's banker") is seen hung from a bridge. The plot to kill Michael during the performance at the opera house goes wrong and the action spills out onto the front steps. The assassin shoots and wounds Michael but is shot dead by Vincent. Mary, however, has been hit by a bullet meant for her father and collapses dead in front of him. Michael utters a profound cry of loss and despair.

The scene on the steps dissolves into a reprise of the dance between father and daughter that took place at the opening of the film, followed by a montage of dance scenes – Michael with Apollonia, Michael with Kay – which dissolve in turn to images of a dying Michael, a very old man, alone in the Sicilian sunshine.

COPPOLA: A BRIEF BIOGRAPHY

The public image of Coppola the artist tends, probably more than other film directors, to converge around the figure of the man himself. Coppola's career is often read like Orson Welles's – as an emblem of conflict between an independent genius and the powerful and ultimately repressive force of the industry. The biographical record is well established and often repeated. The second son of Carmine and Italia Coppola, Francis Coppola was born in Detroit in 1939. Carmine Coppola was a professional musician, a concert flautist, composer, and conductor, who played under Toscanini in the NBC Symphony. Francis, stricken by polio at the age of nine and confined to bed for a year, grew up in the New York City suburbs. He attended Hofstra University where he was an active and indeed much celebrated figure in campus theater, graduating in 1959. He enrolled at the UCLA Film School where he won writing awards, met many of his friends and collaborators (mostly from USC), and found his first professional work in "the nudies." His apprenticeship at twenty-three began with Roger Corman, "King of the B's," who financed his first commercial feature, *Dementia 13* (1963). While working for Warner–Seven Arts he wrote, and in 1970 received an Academy award for, the script of *Patton*. Three films later (two small, independent-minded films and a Hollywood musical), in 1970, at the age of thirty-one he was offered *The Godfather*.

In 1969 while on the road in Nebraska shooting *The Rain People* from his original script (an identity story of a woman who "misplaces her children"), Coppola searched for a way to give institutional form to his idea of independent film making. From 1969 to the mid-1990s, Zoetrope was the public face and form of Coppola's attempt to merge personal, auteurist film making with an ensemble cast with a new type of studio film and associated distribution. The principal drama of Coppola's artistic life has been the effort to make this vision a functioning reality. With money from Warner Brothers, in 1969 Coppola set up a small, highly equipped studio in San Francisco for development. On seeing Lucas's *THX-1138* and the scripts for *Apocalypse Now* and *The Conversation*, Warner asked for its money back. However, the Zoetrope concept of the return of artistic control of film making to film makers and the real efforts he made in that direction was the basis of his reputation as the godfather of the New Hollywood.

In the 1970s Coppola reached international stature and acclaim by directing four highly successful films: *The Godfather* (1972) and *The Godfather Part II* (1974) (both at Paramount); the *Conversation* (1974), an art film about electronic bugging; and his Vietnam film, *Apocalypse Now* (1979), done with United Artists. The two *Godfather* films raised Coppola to the heights of the industry, becoming among the most profitable and acclaimed films of the era. Both films won "Best Picture." *Godfather Part II* earned Coppola "Best Director" in 1974. In the same year, *The Conversation* earned the "Best Picture" award at the Cannes Film Festival, and a few years later *Apocalypse Now* was nominated for eight Academy Awards.

In 1979 Coppola was at the peak of his reputation. His record of financial and artistic success was legend. He was seen as a flamboyant, even reckless, risk taker, an innovative technological visionary, a devotee of film as an international art, the patriarch of the "Auteur Renaissance" in Hollywood, and an ambitious mogul ready and committed to change Hollywood. The testing of the limits of his personal physical endurance and even sanity in the shoot of *Apocalypse Now* consolidated his image not only as the godfather of blockbusters – he produced one of the most successful movies of all time – but the crazed auteur protagonist of "the ultimate movie."

With his purchase of Hollywood General Studios in 1980, Coppola's entrepreneurial ambitions became embroiled in a financial morass that led eventually at the end of the decade to personal bankruptcy and artistic decline. At the start, the Zoetrope spirit and its believers were ensconced at the Hollywood studio. Coppola distributed – in magnificent style – a number of foreign classics, including Abel Gance's *Napoleon*. He distributed new work by leading European and Japanese directors and assisted and supported new productions by old friends. The business concept behind Zoetrope was to gain greater control over the film-making process by financing development of new projects with loans secured by future revenues. Coppola was studio artistic director and all-round godfather. But, in addition, he was committed to pay for new projects and maintain the staff with his own money. In taking on *One from the Heart* (1980), Coppola, an enthusiast of the coming communications "revolution" was betting that the new technologies, in particular video, would profoundly alter the technological basis of film production. Innovation proved to be expensive. On release, the film recouped only a small fraction of its high cost. Development of key projects faltered or collapsed, and when Coppola became producer and sought additional loans, costs grew. The large debts incurred for setting up the studio and the development of expensive creative projects was only half-satisfied by the bank-ordered sale of the studio in 1984. The Zoetrope experiment of institutionalizing his pioneering new way had collapsed.

In the second half of the 1980s, Coppola moved again in the two directions that had defined his artistic personality – toward small experimental works in locations distant from Hollywood (the black-and-white *Rumble Fish*, for example) and works as a director-for-hire at established studios. Critical opinion had it that he brought skill as a craftsman but little in the way of feeling to these Hollywood projects. *Peggy Sue Got Married* (1986), a back-to-the-future story set in 1960, was his biggest hit of the decade. *Tucker: The Man and His Dream* (1988), the story of a startup, independent automobile manufacturer of the 1950s who contended with Detroit – and lost – was generally understood as a personal allegory of creativity and survival. In 1990 he completed *The Godfather Part III* and subsequently turned to directing and to producing faithful adaptations of works of classic horror. After he declared personal and corporate bankruptcy in 1992, the considerable profits from *Bram Stoker's Dracula* allowed Coppola to clear his debts and move on.

THE *GODFATHER* FILMS IN CONTEXT

The crime genre is a traditional, long-standing form of American film making. The genre shows a different face according to the ways it adapts to changing social circumstances. By delineating the urban boundaries of the lawful, the genre indicates the possibilities and limits of living and representing American life outside the law. Jack Shadoian, in his *Dreams and Deadends*, is right to say that the genre is the central paradigm for investigating the inherent contradictions of the American dream of success.

The genre is structured by a fundamental antagonism – between the gangster and the law. The result, violence – of a specific kind – is the signature gesture of the genre. In the classic form, the law was ultimately legitimate and governed the perspective on the story. In the Vietnam era, however, the values attached to the conflict between the two parties were reversed. In *Bonnie and Clyde* (1967), for example, audience identification with the outlaw position of the protagonists was legimated and the couple mythologized by the force of the violence directed against them. The distinctive place of the *Godfather* films in the evolution of the Vietnam era crime genre was its displacement of the classical conflict in an essentially conservative direction by reinstating the Church as the arbiter of justice. In these films the police and legal apparatus have been rendered as incidental – either ineffective or corrupt – present only at the periphery of the action. Legitimate civil authority is nearly invisible, simply an external reference for the criminal enterprise. The opposition between the gangster and the law as the animating conflict of the genre has dissolved. The dramatic locus shifted in the trilogy to a conflict among criminal gangs.

The social world created by the *Godfather* films is that of an aggregation of cooperating, competitive criminal families that requires the implicit sanction of the legitimate world. The first two films bring together and interlock two stories – the struggle over control of the changing postwar, Italian-American underworld and, second, the management of the problem of generational succession – that is passing control within one family from father to the right son. In this world the gang is the family and the family the operative unit in war for self-preservation and expansion. The fortified compound is its physical emblem. Strategic assets must be defended and preserved. Self-preservation requires the men of the family to take their place within the patriarchal/military order. Women occupy a space apart. Loyalty to the family is the fundamental ethic. Family affiliation can take several forms: relations by blood, by marriage, and by employment. Breach of the law of loyalty is punishable by death.

Dramatic action in this world can be initiated by a challenge from without (Sollozzo wants to kill the Don to get access to his official assets, the judges, etc.) or by defection and deceit from within (Carlo betrays Sonny, Fredo betrays Michael). Murder and intrigue for business advantage are the principal mechanisms by which this world moves. In the *Godfather* films the law of the civil order (police and so on) has been replaced by the iron law of familial self-preservation in the name of the father. This is why the story of Michael the son is so important: it leads to the problem of paternal succession, to the problem of power, and finally to the quest for redemption.

As the protagonist of the trilogy, Michael Corleone is the modern successor to the prewar ways of his father. With both a war experience and a college degree, he figures a new era in the world of business signaled by his move from New York to Las Vegas. Like his father, however, Michael's rise to power and his operational legitimacy is founded on a murder. He must still operate between the old (Sicily) and the new (America). The transformation of his personality ("That's my family, Kay, not me") toward ruthlessness is, however, a requirement to occupy his future position. The murder is a decisive, calculated move, the defense of the father at the hospital innovative and strategic. His sexuality is bound to the norms of the family. As patriarch he assumes the responsibility to protect the family (he must be circumspect and reasonable), and in the name of the family, Michael destroys it.

Though violence is by no means exclusive to the crime genre, the genre's conventions take on special cultural weight and significance. Traditionally, the central violent action of the classic form of the genre involved santioned agents of the law, that is to say professionals, doing a job. Killing by lawmen was sanctioned in the name of the social order and justified by criminals often in the name of evasion. The violence of the *Godfather* films, however, does not take place within that sanctioned framework. Rather, it takes place almost wholly within the criminal underworld (even when the underworld as in *Part III* is an elevated one) and takes two principal forms – violence as a business strategy and part of a rational calculation with a wholly secular justification (Sollozzo: "Blood is a big expense."), and the second: killing as punishment for betrayal of family loyalty. There are degrees of violation and sanction. At the ultimate level, killing of blood relatives (Fredo), is not a *crime* but a *sin* that only the Church can mediate.

In the world of the *Godfathers*, violence is not arbitrary or meaningless. On the contrary, it is a constituent part of a scheme of justice rooted in social necessity. Indeed, the social fabric of the film is constituted by violence. The *Godfather* films, in other words, treat violence as a necessary fact and as part of the social contract that creates the world. Though violence is often graphic (Luca Brazzi's strangulation), it is never gratuitous. It functions clearly in a strategic plan and its ethical meaning is never obscured. Sonny's close-up, bloody death by machine gun on the road followed by a kick to the head is a telling emblem of gangland viciousness. By contrast, Michael's killing of Fredo as he recites his Hail Marys at a great distance carries with it the sense of a moral transgression. Subsequently, Michael suffers. In the *Godfather* films the Church replaces civil law as the ultimate arbiter of justice. Moreover, the Church is a law above the family. Between the presentation of violence as social fact and as religious transgression, is an aesthetic order, evident, for example, in the dramatic culmination of *The Godfather Part III*, which is cast in an operatic mode. Under Coppola's direction, violence is part of an aesthetic whole and figures importantly in a moral vision on the historical world he represents.

THE ESSAYS

The commentary and criticism on Coppola is extensive. There are literally thousands of items – including Web pages, newspaper articles, essays, books, interviews, films, and so on. The most up-to-date published coverage of his career as a whole is Peter Cowie's *Coppola: A Biography*. For historical perspective, we are reprinting here, as appendixes, articles published at the time the films first appeared: William Pechter's "Keeping Up with the Corleones" (1972) and David Denby's "The Two Godfathers" (1976), supplemented with a selected part of a wide-ranging interview with Coppola published shortly after the release of *The Godfather Part II*. The main part of this book, and its reason for being, are the five remarkable, original chapters by leading American film scholars.

Jon Lewis's chapter, "If History Has Taught Us Anything . . . ," provides a perspective on the place of the *Godfather* films in the post-1960s Hollywood studio system. In a vivid style of writing that pictures the lives, attitudes, motivations, and argot of the people involved, Lewis shows how the behind-the-scenes business cirscumstances of the industry and its key players shaped the *Godfather* films. Lewis shows how these films got made and why they are the way they are. The chapter is a case study of a certain kind of collaborative, Hollywood-style film making – the struggle between a young, strong-willed director with an original creative vision and the array of powerful financial interests. For Lewis, the forcefulness and self-assertation of the director in the board room, on the set, and in his public statements was a demonstration of the viability of the "auteur theory" at this uncertain moment in Hollywood history. The power to create the film with a certain cast and style lay principally, but by no means exclusively, with the director. At points the vagaries of ego and price, especially in casting, required a change of plans. Dramatic confirmation and ratification of the importance of the creative individual in the system could be seen in the striking success of these films with both audiences and critics. Coppola was the linchpin of a notable change in the post-1960s studio system: he demonstrated that a personal artistic vision could be, and might even be necessary to, the foundation of enormous financial success, one that inaugurated the Hollywood blockbuster syndrome. The Director's Company, formed to take stock of prominent young directors, was one of a long line of efforts to capitalize on directorial talent in a studio setting. The prestige of Coppola's initial achievement and the amount of money he made for the studio were measures of his impact and guaranteed his control of *Parts II* and *III*.

For Alessandro Camon, Mafia conduct and its meaning are intimately linked to its mythology, a mythology profoundly changed by the movies. Originally rooted in protection of landowners against possible peasant appropriation of land, over time the Mafia organization became the vehicle both for the protection of property held by aristocrats and for mobility for the underprivileged. The Mafia ethic is a deeply social one concerned with the reproduction of the importance of hereditary status and, in particular, solidifying the bond between father and son. Its patriarchal foundation and the associated paradigm of masculinity – of silence, honor, and protection – governed the relations of men and women in the family. It brought together in an unstable balance two antagonistic attitudes – deep familial devotion and ruthless extermination of enemies in the name of the family.

The acculturation of this Sicilian-originated myth and its translation into popular culture, and into the *Godfather* films in particular, necessarily required adaptation. In America, the celebration of the traditional ethic underwent a cultural displacement that ultimately took the form of disillusionment with its progressive adulteration. The myth was caught between the forces of preservation and assimilation. The mainstreaming of the Mafia myth within a commodity culture profoundly altered its traditional contours and justifications. Popularization of what had been secret, making it public, turned it into spectacle. The *Godfather* films represented a decisive moment in this process of acculturation and disintegration. The films, novels, and television serials put the Mafia code of silence into play, significantly changed the Mafia outlook on itself, and helped move forward crime itself as a journalistic and aesthetic commodity. While undergoing an erosion of its justification, the Mafia became a media creation in its own right. Camon not only provides us with an anatomy of the paradoxes of this mythology, the polarities of its orientation, but in the outline of its historical evolution, shows how and why Mafia mythology has been adapted to modern forms of mass entertainment.

Vera Dika's analysis of the transformation of the image of the Italian criminal and her account of its function as a kind of stereotype provides a view of the *Godfather* films as an American cultural phenomenon. Mafia, she points out, is not a code of lawlessness. Originally, the necessity of the Mafia code lay in the need for a means of protection of the poor or powerless from the injustice of landlords. In *The Godfather,* the Mafia functions by a return to the traditional code to arbitrate injustice and provide protection. The emphasis in the first film especially and in *Godfather Part II* in the retrospective sections is on the chivalrous code of the old Godfather and his Old World ways – a treatment that diminishes his association with crime. The films merge this ethic with a system of family values. Much of the violence in the films is justified by the masculinist ethic in defense of family. By setting the story in the immigrant past and authenticating it with a wealth of historical detail and associated nostalgia, Coppola provided his audience with a reality substitute – an imaginative vehicle for occluding and reworking contemporary anxiety and discontent with the changes in America wrought by the Vietnam war. The film's image of a powerful American success story is invested in the complex aesthetics of nostalgia. The film presents a historical past with the possibility of traditional honor pictured, to be sure, in the process of deteriorating under the pressure of American life. The cinematic image of solitary, masculine power was in fact, Dika argues, a filmic substitute for an actual loss – that of the family, the nation, and even the integrity of the individual in the Vietnam era. *The Godfather* and *The Godfather Part II* are, moreover, a fantasy covering over and transforming lost white male privilege from a perspective very much like the men who made the film. "Italianicity," the term Dika gives to a cluster of cultural traits, is a cinematic reconstruction of the genre that grounded the social world of the film in many believable, "authentic" details of period and place. This reconstruction and recasting worked, one might say, for ideological ends. *Part III* for Dika is a self-conscious criticism of the enabling mythology that supports *I and II*. Dika's chapter offers a cultural analysis of the films' popularity and reads the Italian connection as a refashioned emblem of an American past recounted in the postmodern mode of nostalgia.

Glenn Man's chapter on genre and ideology investigates the contradictory makeup of the crime genre. He regards the genre as formed by the play of a complex set of oppositions – individual/society – being the principal one. In the classic form, the criminal had to give way, usually by death, to the insistence on social order regulated by the law. By the 1960s, however, as in *Bonnie and Clyde,* the perspective of the narration sided with the outsiders, identified with their vitality, and experienced the violence of establishment repression. The classical valences of the opposition – individual/society – were subject to reversal. For Man, *The Godfather* puts forward a positive picture of the family as the fundamental term of social order. But insofar as the family is a metaphor for the social order more generally, the film is an implicit criticism of that order. Coppola's dramatization of Michael's hypocrisy at the very end of the film makes this criticism evident. Through romanticization of the Vito/Michael bond, the film masks criticism of the dominant economic mode in America – rampant capitalism. *The Godfather Part II,* however, makes this criticism overt. It self-consciously works to deromanticize Michael by making more explicit the analogy between the family and the economy as models of social order. Coppola goes further in showing that the cause of Michael's moral disintegration is inseparable from his struggle for social dominance through elimination of his competitors or any other agent (Fredo, for example) that cooperates with them. Man sees the principal impulse in *The Godfather Part II* as a frontal criticism of the ideology of capitalistic self-justification. Michael comes to mirror the world the family inhabits – that is to say, the predatory destructive violence of Mafia business. The paramount exponent of family order becomes the chief architect of its destruction. *Godfather Part III* continues the critical outlook of *Part II* and expands the scope of venality to the "legitimate" world of international high finance. Michael's efforts to atone for his sins can only be pursued within the Church, which is itself subject to fraud and murder. Though sincere in his desire for redemption, he cannot escape from a world made corrupt by the practitioners of modern business. His attempt at redemption through familial restoration in that world is doomed to failure. His son refuses to follow his father by insisting on a career in music, and his daughter is killed by bullets intended for him. Man treats Coppola's ideological roots as an analysis and confrontation with the contradictions inherent in the psychical and ethical requirements of modern big business. The films stand as major critical statements of the American way of life by staging a drama that shows the price of such huge success.

Naomi Greene in "Family Ceremonies: or, Opera in the *Godfather* Films" argues that in both form and spirit the films are similar to the great works of nineteenth-century Italian opera. She identifies several fundamental formal, operatic strategies that constitute the architecture of the trilogy. They include the films' insistence on the role of the chorus to form and enlarge the drama; the role of musical leitmotifs as a regular reminder of what went before; the use of structural repetition and of comparison from film to film to mark events and to signal change (for example, the ceremonial events that open all three films); the inclination to treat events that provoke extreme emotion in ways that skirt melodrama. But the principal operatic strategy she identifies in the trilogy is the juxtaposition of the ceremonial and the everyday, the sacred and the profane. This contrast is especially evident in scenes of violence where a life is taken. Greene identifies this essential aesthetic as the transformation of the everyday through operatic means, usually liturgical in content, toward the ceremonial. This operatic mode of representation of events runs throughout the films and serves to show how far, morally, Michael has fallen. But in addition, the trilogy draws on operatic narrative and theme to enlarge the resonance of the subject – in particular by the use and reference to works of Mascagni and Verdi. The music of *Cavalleria Rusticana* defines the end of *Godfather Part III*. Likewise, Verdi's *Rigoletto,* a story of the inadvertent murder of a daughter through the intrigues of the father, informs and gives import to the ending of the trilogy. Finally, Greene argues, inasmuch as Verdi's operas were works involving the fate of a nation, the historical scope makes the subject of the *Godfather* films nothing less than the American experience in this century, and like Italian opera, gives Coppola the perspective to witness and evaluate its moral significance. Coppola can be viewed, Greene argues, as the inheritor in terms of both theme and mode of a powerful operatic tradition.

1 If History Has Taught Us Anything . . . Francis Coppola, Paramount Studios, and *The Godfather Parts I, II,* and *III*

In March 1970, Hollywood unemployment reached 42.8 percent, an all-time high.[1] Despite a new ratings code and the increasingly sophisticated use of market research, theatrical films ran a distant second to the record industry in terms of annual gross revenues. Rising short-term interest rates and a seeming inability to comprehend the late-sixties mass audience contributed to what the trades characterized as a box office crisis. In response to this crisis, the studios increased production; by the summer of 1970, there was more than $100 million worth of negative in general release, the most ever.[2]

The studios' decision to flood the market with product was misguided. Few films in 1970 made money, and even those that did seemed to have little in common. The box office leaders for the year were, in order, the disaster-thriller *Airport,* the *auteur*-comedy *Mash, Patton* (scripted by Francis Coppola), the topical *Bob, Carol, Ted and Alice* and *Woodstock,* and the big-budget musical *Hello Dolly.* Of all the successful releases, only *Airport* qualified as a blockbuster and, more importantly, only *Airport* seemed like something the studios could easily reproduce.

In 1970, Paramount ranked ninth in the industry, behind the six other majors and two independents, National General and Cinerama.[3] The big news at Paramount at the time was its parent company Gulf & Western's various attempts to unload the legendary Melrose Avenue Paramount production facility, a move at one point blocked only by Gulf & Western's inability to get an adjacent property – a cemetary – rezoned.[4]

Unable to sell the property, Gulf & Western CEO Charles Bluhdorn staked the studio's future on the expertise of three men in their early thirties: Hollywood veteran Stanley Jaffe, sales and advertising expert Frank Yablans, and a former actor and fashion industry executive, Robert Evans. Jaffe, the studio chief, seems in retrospect the least noteworthy, though his was the most familar name at the time. Indeed, Jaffe was out before he had the chance to do much, clearing the way for Yablans, who became the first in what is now a long list of former marketing executives to take over a studio.

In addition to his marketing and exhibition expertise, by the time he joined Paramount, Yablans had earned a reputation as a cost-conscious executive with a willingness to "get tough" with exhibitors and the various industry guilds,[5] first at Disney and then at Filmways. While a vice-president at Paramount, Yablans helped Bluhdorn downsize the studio operation, at one point firing over 1,100 employees at Paramount and MCA/Universal's jointly held distribution company, Cinema International.[6] As president, Yablans promised to cut production costs to an average of $2.5 million a picture[7] and to better diversify Paramount by working to effect a reversal of the Consent Decree, which, after World War II, had prevented the studios from controlling exhibition venues.[8]

Evans was named production chief of Paramount in 1967, and though he and Yablans got along very well, the two men were very different philosophically. Unlike Yablans, Evans was a production-oriented executive and, again unlike his boss, he had little practical experience before taking the job. When Bluhdorn formally announced the hiring of Evans as the new production chief at the studio, the trades excoriated him, labeling the move "Bluhdorn's Folly" and "Bluhdorn's Blow Job."[9] But Bluhdorn proved them all wrong; Evans was the perfect man for the job.

With Evans in charge of production, Paramount dramatically increased its importance in the Gulf & Western family of companies, upping its share of the multinational's annual revenues from 5 percent in 1967 to almost 50 percent in 1976. Twice in the first three years of the decade, the studio posted the number one box office film for the year – *Love Story* in 1971 and then *The Godfather* the following year. Both projects originated with and were developed by Evans.[10]

Evans's method of acquiring these two big properties was unusual and particularly smart. With regard to *Love Story*, Evans advanced $25,000 to publisher Harper & Row to help finance a 25,000-copy first printing of the novel.[11] In exchange for the investment – which dramatically changed the way the publishing house promoted the book – Evans received an option on the novel before it was a best-seller. Paramount produced the movie version of *Love Story* in 1971, and the picture grossed in excess of $50 million domestically, accounting for roughly a third of Paramount Studios' gross revenues for the year and earning over three times as much as the year's number two film, Arthur Penn's *Little Big Man*. The dramatic box office success of *Love Story* sent a clear message to the rest of the industry that one film by itself could save a studio.

Evans moved just as quickly (and just as early) to acquire the screen rights to *The Godfather*. As Evans tells the story in his 1994 memoir, *The Kid Stays in the Picture*, in the spring of 1968, Mario Puzo came to him with "fifty or sixty rumpled pages" of a book tentatively titled *Mafia*. At the time, according to Evans, Puzo owed bookies approximately $10,000 he didn't have. Evans advanced Puzo $12,500 and in exchange virtually stole the screen rights to one of the biggest novels of the decade.

An alternative version of Evans's colorful story about how Paramount first optioned *The Godfather* is told by Coppola biographer Peter Cowie. As Cowie tells it, by the time Puzo approached Paramount, he had already received a $5,000 advance from and had contracted to write the novel for GP Putnam & Sons. Hoping to presell the movie rights to the book, Puzo took sixty pages of an early draft of the novel to George Wieser, a story editor at Paramount, who liked it because he thought it "read like a Harold

Robbins best seller." Wieser then took the property to Evans and his assistant, Peter Bart. At first Evans wasn't interested because the studio had just lost money on Martin Ritt's gangster picture, *The Brotherhood.* But Wieser persisted and eventually Evans agreed to purchase an option for the low-ball figure of $12,500.[12] After purchasing the option, Evans began to develop the project. But he did so cautiously, still unconvinced that there would be an audience for a movie about organized crime.

It wasn't until Evans began to fear that the project might be taken away from him – by actor Burt Lancaster – that he began to commit to the film. In 1970, Lancaster's production company approached the studio and offered to participate in the financing of the production as long as Lancaster got to star in the film. Evans opposed making a deal with Lancaster for a couple of reasons; he didn't think the actor was right for the title role, but more importantly, he did not want to diminish studio profit interest in the project by selling off a piece of it to an independent production company.

To a large extent, Coppola owes his career to Lancaster, and Evans and Paramount owe their 1970s turnaround to a series of spurned offers and lost arguments in the early development of the picture. When Peter Bart first suggested to Evans that they hire Francis Coppola to direct *The Godfather,* Evans found the idea preposterous. Coppola had by that point in time directed one B movie *(Dementia 13)* and three studio films *(You're a Big Boy Now, The Rain People,* and *Finian's Rainbow),* none of which did well at the box office. Moreover, Coppola had a reputation for playing fast and loose with studio funds; in 1969 he took $600,000 in development money from Warner Brothers and spent it all on state-of-the-art production equipment. When the studio rejected all of his (and his fledgling company, American Zoetrope's) projects and asked for their money back, Coppola had to tell them the money was gone. In order to pay Warner back, Coppola hired himself out to shoot television commercials and industrial films, but so considerable was his debt to Warner that when rumors circulated that Paramount intended to offer Coppola the chance to direct *The Godfather*, Warner Brothers executives called Evans to tell him that he might as well send the check to them.

Bart claims that unlike Evans he appreciated Coppola's talent from the start. As an industry journalist, Bart had met Coppola in San Francisco and found him to be "an extraordinarily bright person" who wrote "fabulous screenplays." But despite Bart's enthusiasm and confidence, the studio's decision to hire Coppola had less to do with Bart's appreciation of the young director's talent than with Evans's resolve to keep the project out of Burt Lancaster's hands and his seeming inability to interest a single mainstream action director in the picture. In Coppola's favor was the fact that he was Italian-American and, because he was so deeply in debt, he could be hired cheaply.[13]

Evans finally agreed to offer the job to Coppola only after Richard Brooks, Constantin Costa-Gavras, Elia Kazan, Arthur Penn,[14] Franklin Schaffner, Fred Zinneman, Lewis Gilbert, and Peter Yates[15] turned him down. Many of the directors declined Evans's offers because they objected to the ways in which the script and the novel glorified organized crime. Several others expressed concern about being associated with a potentially incendiary ethnic picture. In the meantime, Bart continued to lobby for Coppola, at one point telling Evans that if he ever wanted to get the film made, he would eventually have to choose between Coppola and Lancaster.[16] In order to maintain studio control over the project, Evans decided to follow Bart's advice and made an offer to Coppola. But to his astonishment, Coppola was inclined to refuse, not because of the film's politics but because he had no interest in directing a mainstream genre picture. Legend has it that it was Coppola's friend, George Lucas, who finally convinced him to accept Evans's offer, arguing that if he directed *The Godfather* he would never have to make another commercial film again.

After three days of negotiations with the studio, Coppola finally took Lucas's advice and provisionally agreed, as long as, in Bart's recounting of Coppola's terms, "it's not a film about organized gangsters, but a family chronicle. A metaphor for capitalism in

America."[17] Evans found Coppola's concept for the film ridiculous, even pretentious. But, confident that the studio's final cut left *him* in control of the picture, Evans had a contract drawn up and Coppola signed for $150,000 plus 7.5 percent of the net to direct the picture.

Evans's notion that he could control Coppola was immediately put to the test when Coppola decided to cast Al Pacino as Michael Corleone. Evans thought Pacino was too short and that all three of his screen tests were awful. Coppola steadfastly held that Pacino was the only actor for the part. According to Evans, he finally agreed to hire Pacino on the condition that Coppola agree to cast James Caan as Sonny, even though Coppola had already hired an Italian actor, Carmine Carridi, for the part.

After Coppola agreed to cast Caan, Evans made the offer to Pacino. But, by then, Pacino had signed with MGM to appear in *The Gang That Couldn't Shoot Straight*. In 1971, MGM was owned by Las Vegas billionaire Kirk Kerkorian and was run by James Aubrey, a notoriously difficult character to deal with. According to Evans, in order to keep Coppola happy, he asked his friend, the reputed Mafia lawyer Sidney Korshak,[18] to help him out with Aubrey. As Evans tells the story, twenty minutes after hanging up with Korshak, Aubrey called Evans: "You no-good motherfucker, cocksucker. I'll get you for this. . . . The midget's [Pacino's] yours." According to Evans, Korshak called Aubrey's boss, suggesting that he release Pacino from his contract. Evans asked Korshak what he had said to convince Kerkorian to cooperate and Korshak responded: "I asked him if he wanted to finish building his hotel."[19]

Evans also opposed Coppola's plan to cast Marlon Brando in the title role. Legend has it that after lengthy discussion, Coppola finally sold Evans on Brando by shooting a silent screen test in which the actor stuffed his cheeks with cotton to create the image of the older, heavier Don Corleone. When Brando signed on, he agreed to a strange but ultimately lucrative back-end deal in which he received only $50,000 up front. The balance of his compensation package depended on how well the film did at the box office. If the picture crossed the $50 million mark – as only three or four films had in the history of the business – significant incentives kicked in and Brando's percentage of the gross increased incrementally. By the end of 1972, Brando was contracted to receive almost 6 percent of the movie's $81 million gross.[20]

By the time the casting was complete and principal photography had begun, Evans and Coppola had become enemies and it is a rift that has persisted to this day.[21] In a 1975 *Playboy* interview, Coppola told William Murry that "a lot of energy that went into *[The Godfather]* went into simply trying to convince the people who held the power [read here, Evans] to let [me] do the film [my] way."[22] Almost ten years later, as he began work on the screenplay for Evans's production of *The Cotton Club,* Coppola told another interviewer: "I'm terrified of being in a situation where I have people second-guessing me. If I have to fight for everything, like I had to fight for Al Pacino and Marlon Brando, I don't have the energy anymore."[23]

In a 1984 interview, Evans told his side of the story. According to Evans, Coppola's final cut of *The Godfather* "looked like a section out of [the television show] *The Untouchables*"; it was so bad, Evans had to recut and "[change] the picture around entirely."[24] In his 1994 memoir, Evans recounts an exchange of telegrams between the two men in mid-December 1983. The first, unsigned but supposedly sent by Coppola, read as follows: "Dear Bob Evans, I've been a real gentleman regarding your claims of involvement in *The Godfather.* I've never talked about your throwing out the Nino Rota music, your barring the casting of Pacino and Brando, etc. But continually your stupid babbling about cutting *The Godfather* comes back and angers me for its ridiculous pomposity."[25] The second telegram was sent and signed by Evans the following day: "Thank you for your charming cable. I cannot imagine what prompted this venemous diatribe. I am both annoyed and exasperated by your fallacious accusations. . . . I am affronted by your gall in daring to send this Machiavellian epistle. The content of which is not only ludicrous, but totally misrepresents the truth."[26]

Given that *The Godfather* has become something of a legendary American *auteur* picture – one that is generally and justifiably credited with starting the so-called *auteur* renaissance in the 1970s – Evans's challenge to Coppola's authority over *The Godfather* seems significant beyond their perhaps petty (but nonetheless fascinating) feud. Evans after all had final cut on the film, and according to his assistant, Peter Bart, he exercised that right and saved the picture. *"The Godfather* was a seminal experience," Bart argues, "in that Evans was dissatisfied with Francis Coppola's cut and spent months working round the clock with him on the film, even postponing its release date. Now the gossip in town was that Evans was intruding on the prerogatives of young filmmakers. The reality was quite the opposite: I watched as a superbly shot but ineptly put together film was transformed into a masterpiece."[27]

Though both men remain bitter about who exactly cut the movie, Evans and Coppola agree that it is Evans's and not Coppola's ending that audiences saw in 1972. Coppola had shot and hoped to use a final scene of Kay in church lighting a candle for Michael's sins. The film ends instead as the door slowly closes in Kay's face; first we get a glimpse of Michael's lieutenants kissing his ring and then Kay's enigmatic look of despair. Coppola's original ending returns us to the film's thematic conflation of family and religion and Michael's betrayal of both in his seizure of power. Evans's ending accounts only for Michael's power and Kay's growing irrelevance in his life.

The Coppola–Evans feud was only one of several on-the-set battles during the production of the *The Godfather*. After Coppola finished shooting the restaurant scene in which Michael gets revenge against Solozzo and the crooked policeman who broke his jaw, Aram Avakian, the film's original editor, called Evans to tell him that the film "wouldn't cut," that Coppola had "no idea what continuity means." To check out Avakian's accusations – perhaps secretly hoping they were true – Evans hired a second editor, Peter Zinner, who much to Evans's surprise said that the scene was terrific. Evans realized then that Avakian was lobbying for Coppola's job and fired him and several other key production personnel.[28]

Although the mass firings seemed to indicate that Coppola finally had Evans's support, the executive's next move suggested the opposite. After the Avakian episode, Evans hired Elia Kazan to stand by in case he eventually had to replace Coppola. In conversation with Peter Cowie, Coppola recalled the anxiety he felt at the time: "I kept dreaming that Kazan would arrive on the set and would say to me, 'Uh Francis, I've been asked to . . .' But Marlon, who knew about this, was very supportive and said he would not continue to work on the film if I was fired."[29]

The battle between Coppola and Evans took no one in the industry by surprise, and in context, to steal a line from the movie, for Evans at least, it wasn't personal, it was business. Approximately a year before the release of *The Godfather*, under the page 1 *Variety* headline, "Cut Directors Down to Size," Evans announced his (and Paramount's) intention to "become [more] involved in product on a creative basis," to "be close[r] to the script development, the casting and the final cuts." If writers and directors didn't like his rules, Evans bristled, "they should stay away."[30]

Evans's remarks were, at the time, directed specifically at Elaine May, the writer-director of the Paramount production, *A New Leaf*. At the time, May claimed that Evans had "drastically changed" her work and filed suit in federal court in order to enjoin the release of the film. Film maker Arthur Penn entered the fray on May's behalf, as did British cineaste Anthony Harvey, who remarked that the only reason Evans was so bold was that he had just made so much money with *Love Story*.[31] Evans no doubt agreed with Harvey about the importance of *Love Story* to his and Paramount's decision to "deflate 'big me' directors;"[32] in Hollywood you are only as good as your last film, and at the time Evans would not have had it any other way.

The choice of Coppola to direct *The Godfather* seemed consistent with this hands-on production policy. At the time Evans guessed that he would have more success pushing around a relatively inexperienced director like Coppola than someone like Yates or Costa-Gavras. Evans also planned to use Coppola to allay concern about how the studio planned to portray the Mafia. As expected, objections to the shooting script were raised early on, but Coppola, a relative unknown at the time, remained in the background, and Evans was forced to deal with the situation on his own. Even before the start of principal photography, negotiations between *Godfather* producer Al Ruddy and the New York chapter of the Italian-American Civil Rights League were well under way. The result of these often contentious negotiations ultimately proved embarrassing for both sides and served only to reinforce the absurdity of the studio's and the League's claims of good intentions and mutual respect.

In the March 20, 1971, edition of the *New York Times,* Ruddy announced that, after lengthy negotiations with the Italian-American Civil Rights League, Paramount had agreed to eliminate all references to the Mafia and Cosa Nostra from the screenplay. In a related story, the *Times* reported that then U.S. Attorney General John Mitchell, apparently moved by Ruddy's sensitivity, had decided to follow suit and ordered the Justice Department to stop using the terms as well. In place of Mafia and Cosa Nostra, Ruddy inserted "the five families."

Puzo was unavailable for comment – he was at the Duke University weight-reduction clinic – but at the time Grace Lichtenstein for the *Times* surmised that Puzo would not have approved. She pointed out that both words appear frequently in the novel and that, by 1971, there had been more than 700,000 hardcover editions and 3 million paperback copies sold. Moreover, in 1967, Puzo, himself an Italian-American, wrote: "Most of the operators in organized crime in this country will bleed Italian blood. That fact must be accepted . . . such bodies as the Italian American pressure groups . . . do everyone concerned a great disservice."[33]

At first, Evans publically supported Ruddy's deal with the Italian-American Civil Rights League. It provided some free, positive, prerelease publicity, and moreover, it was hardly an unusual situation. During the 1970 Paramount production of Philip Roth's *Goodbye Columbus,* the studio negotiated with various Jewish-American interest groups. "We get a lot of flack from all kinds of groups," a spokesman for Gulf & Western told the *Times.* "Hundreds of pressure groups come to us all the time."[34]

But although Paramount's capitulation to the League bought

the studio some peace of mind, it led to a surprising and potentially problematic public relations backlash. Three days after Ruddy's announcement regarding his decision to cut Mafia and Cosa Nostra out of the script, a *Times'* editorial quoted New York State Senator John Marchi (from predominantly Italian-American Staten Island), who characterized Ruddy's capitulation to the pressure group as "a monstrous insult to millions upon millions of loyal Americans of Italian extraction." Arguing that Paramount could do Italian Americans a far greater service if it condemned organized crime, Marchi quipped in conclusion: "Yes, Mr. Ruddy, there might just be a Mafia."[35]

One month later, singer Vic Damone used the *Times* to announce his decision to change his mind about playing Johnny Fontaine, the singer-actor (many believe based on Frank Sinatra) whose career is rescued by Don Corleone. Damone charged that the movie was "not in the best interests of Italian-Americans . . . [that] as an American of Italian descent [he] could not in good conscience continue in the role."[36] At the time, it was rumored that Damone backed out under pressure from the mob. Though there was no evidence to support such a contention, wisely, no one at the studio did anything to counter the rumor.

Unhappy with the way Ruddy's "confab" with the Italian-American Civil Rights League had been characterized in the *Times* and elsewhere – especially after a *Times* story revealed that the League's negotiating team included Anthony Colombo, whose father, Joseph Colombo, was at the time "a reputed leader of organized crime in Brooklyn" – Paramount Pictures executives, including Evans, publically scapegoated Ruddy. In a *Variety* piece titled "Par[amount] repudiates Italo-Am. Group Vs. 'Godfather,'" a spokesman for the studio claimed that the meeting and the subsequent accord between Ruddy and the League was "completely unauthorized." Ignoring the fact that the League had first contacted Evans who then dispatched Ruddy to negotiate in his place, the studio added that it planned to "go along" with the deal not because it supported Ruddy (whom the studio characterized as a producer who exceeded his authority) but rather because of John

Mitchell's decision to have the Justice Department stop referring to Mafia and Cosa Nostra as well.[37]

The Godfather was originally scheduled to be a Christmas 1971 release. But because of Evans's various problems with Coppola's rough cut, the studio put off the premiere until March 14, 1972, and its inital nationwide run to March 19. It was a somewhat risky move given the amount of publicity and production money invested in the picture, but as it turned out, the film turned a profit before it played in a single theater,[38] and by the time its first run was over it grossed over $81 million domestically, the most ever to that date, and posted a record twenty-three consecutive weekly grosses in excess of $2 million.

On March 29, 1972, as Paramount came to realize just how big an event the film had become, they ran a ten-page advertisement in *Variety* listing box office grosses across the country where – and it was everywhere – the film posted three-day records, five-day records, and state records.[39] From the start, Paramount highlighted *The Godfather* as more an event than a film, testimony to Yablans's peculiar marketing and distribution expertise. It is at least ironic that such a legendary *auteur* picture was also the first big film in a new era of marketing in Hollywood, the first film at an old studio run by a very new breed of chief executive, one who knew a lot less about movies than he did about money.

Two weeks later, Paramount ran a two-page advertisement featuring excerpts from thirty-nine reviews. But even in this more traditional advertisement, the film's record box office took precedence. In big block letters printed above and below the reviews, the advertisement read: "From city to city, state to state, coast to coast, *The Godfather* is now a phenomenon."[40]

It would be hard to overestimate the impact – at Paramount, on the industry as a whole – of the astonishing box office success of *The Godfather.* How exactly to reproduce that success was a big and difficult question, but the amount of money a studio could earn from a single property seemed changed forever. Through the first six months of 1972, *The Godfather* grossed in excess of $30 million, roughly twice what Paramount's blockbuster *Love Story* earned in the same time period the year before and four times the revenue earned by the number one film (from January to June) in 1970, *Airport*.[41]

The film's success had an immediate impact on Wall Street as well. Within a month of the premiere of *The Godfather*, Gulf & Western stock traded at $44.75 per share, an all-time high. During the week of April 3–10, trading in Gulf & Western was suspended twice, and a 100 percent margin requirement was invoked, both relatively rare Stock Exchange rules designed to stabilize a volatile stock. By year-end, the Paramount Pictures Leisure Division of Gulf & Western posted record pretax operating profits of $31.2 million, up 55 percent from the previous year.[42]

In early December 1972, after the most successful first run in motion picture history, Yablans announced that Paramount planned to pull *The Godfather* from distribution, effective December 31. The plan at the time was to re-release the picture on March 28, 1973, the day after the Academy Awards. It was a somewhat risky move. Both Evans and Yablans remembered the last time they tried a similar strategy and how poorly *Love Story* did in re-release after netting just one minor award, for "Best Score," in 1971.

On Oscar night, *The Godfather* fared a lot better than its predecessor, winning "Best Picture," "Best Actor" (Brando), and "Best Screenplay."[43] *The Godfather* went on to a successful second run and then in an astonishingly lucrative deal, NBC-TV paid the highest price ever for an exclusive single showing of the film on network television. Although its initial and second-run box office and its televsion sale all broke industry records, the best news of all for Paramount was that, thanks to Robert Evans, it owned over 84 percent of the picture and thus did not have to share the wealth with anyone else.

THE GODFATHER PART II

The year-end box office figures for 1972 were difficult for studio executives to accept. Eight films earned more than $10 million and of those eight, five – *The Godfather*, Peter Bogdanovich's *What's Up Doc* and *Last Picture Show*, Stanley Kubrick's *A Clockwork Orange*, and Bob Fosse's *Cabaret* – qualified as *auteur* pictures, or at least as films more or less identified with the man who made them. The remaining three films fell into more traditional industry categories; the number two film for the year, *Fiddler on the Roof* (which grossed less than a third as much as *The Godfather*), was (like *Cabaret*) an adaptation of a popular Broadway musical; *Diamonds Are Forever* was a James Bond picture; and *Dirty Harry* was a star vehicle (for, of course, Clint Eastwood).

As far as studio executives were concerned, the $81 million earned by *The Godfather* was both a good and a bad omen. It seemed to promise a degree of success undreamed of previously,[44] but it did so accompanied by a new and troubling mass-media rhetoric attending the director as star, the director as *auteur*. That a number of other successful films in 1972 were being talked about in much the same way put the studios in a difficult position. The mass audience that had stayed away from their films at the end of the sixties was back. A number of directors seemed to know what the public wanted to see. But how much power could the studios afford to give these directors, and how long would the trend last?

Of all the studio chiefs, Paramount's Frank Yablans was under the least pressure to react to this new trend. By the time the year-end figures were announced, he had already signed Coppola and Puzo to produce a sequel to *The Godfather*. But for some reason – perhaps he was just being greedy, perhaps he really believed all the hype about an *auteur* renaissance – Yablans surprised everyone and began 1973 with a bold and ultimately unlucky move. After examining the box office figures, he entered into a contract with three big-name directors: Coppola, Peter Bogdanovich, and William Friedkin (the director of the Academy Award–winning *The French Connection* and the soon-to-be-released blockbuster, *The Exorcist*).

Yablans decided to call the production unit the Director's Company,[45] and formally announced the arrangement on January 3, 1973, in a press release signed by the studio chief himself.[46] The

directors' contract with Paramount elaborated the following conditions: each of the directors would make three movies during the
following six years – a second version of the contract stipulated
four films in twelve years – and would act as executive producer
on at least one film directed by one of the other company members. In consideration for Paramount's capital investment of $31.5
million, its assurance of creative autonomy within its production
and distribution superstructure, the guarantee of production fund-
ing (without the hassle of pitching ideas to the various studios),
and a 50 percent profit participation on their films, the directors
were obliged to work exclusively at and for Paramount for the
duration of the contract.

For Yablans, the Director's Company was little more than a new
spin on the old Hollywood practice of contracting talent. But that
was not how he chose to promote the deal in the trades. "This is a
familial relationship," Yablans boasted. "What made this deal possible was the degree of simpatico between the directors and the
studio; we're all in our early thirties and we don't have a great
hierarchy."[47] As far as Yablans was concerned, the Director's Company recontextualized *auteurism* within the studio superstructure;
although the deal ceded a modicum of autonomy to three famous
directors, it did so in exchange for what amounted to the directors' capitulation to the studio's primary goal of producing movies
that made money. "They've all gone through their growth
period," Yablans mused, "indulging their esoteric tastes. Coppola
isn't interested in filming a pomegranate growing in the desert.
They're all very commercial now."[48]

But Yablans's optimism was shortlived. First he battled the Gulf
& Western board to transfer control over Coppola's still-unre-
leased *The Godfather Part II* from the studio proper to the Director's
Company unit. The board blocked his plan by simply pointing
out that the studio's purchase of the property – *The Godfather* and
all its sequels and merchandise – preceded the formation of the
unit. Had they agreed to allow Yablans to shift control of *The Godfather Part II* to the Director's Company, the unit would have been
in the black within a year of its formation. When the board

refused to back Yablans's pet project, they undermined his control not only over the three directors but over the studio as well.

All told, only three films were produced under the Director's Company banner: Coppola's *The Conversation* and Peter Bogdanovich's *Paper Moon* and *Daisy Miller*. Only *Paper Moon* made the studio any money. *Daisy Miller* bombed with audiences and critics, and *The Conversation*, a brilliant but esoteric picture that won the Grand Prix at Cannes in 1974 (against some heady competition: Federico Fellini's *Amarcord*, Jacques Tati's *Parade*, Alain Resnais's *Stavisky*, Rainer Werner Fassbinder's *Ali: Fear Eats the Soul*, and Robert Altman's *Thieves Like Us*) and received an Academy Award nomination for "Best Picture," did little business. What troubled Yablans most about *The Conversation* was not that it performed poorly at the box office, but that, at the very moment the studio's future seemed to be riding on *The Godfather Part II*, Coppola seemed disinterested in the very mass audience he had won over two years before.

Whereas Bogdanovich, who maintained a modest record of success in the early seventies, needed the Director's Company as much as it needed him, both Friedkin and Coppola grew too big too fast for the arrangement to make much sense for them. In September 1974, after the release of *The Exorcist* (which broke the box office record set by *The Godfather*), Friedkin became the industry's hottest director and announced his decision to withdraw from the Director's Company in favor of a more conventional arrangement with Universal.[49] Approximately six months earlier, while in production on two films at the same time at Paramount, Coppola similarly lent little support to the Director's Company unit, announcing that after the release of *The Godfather Part II* he intended to leave Los Angeles in order to "shoot eccentric films without worry[ing] whether they will be profitable or not."[50]

In August 1974, Coppola seemed prepared to do just that, purchasing a significant interest in Cinema 5, an independent distribution house.[51] The low-budget line-up slated for release at Cinema 5 included *Apocalypse Now* (to be directed by John Milius, who wrote the original screenplay in the late sixties for Coppola's

American Zoetrope), *The Return of the Black Stallion* (eventually retitled *The Black Stallion,* to be directed by Carroll Ballard), and *Tucker* (to be directed by Coppola).[52]

However Yablans felt about the way two of the Director's Company members contributed to the unit's swift demise, he could ill afford to vent his disappointment in the trades. At the time, Coppola was still working on *The Godfather Part II.* The film was scheduled for release in December 1974 and Yablans needed a hit badly. Paramount fell from number one to number five in 1973 and once again the year-end box office tally offered little in the way of a clear message.[53]

The number one film in 1973 was a B movie with an A cast and budget shot by a little-known studio director – the disaster epic *The Poseidon Adventure,* directed by Ronald Neame, which earned more than twice as much as the number two film of the year, but less than half as much as *The Godfather.* The top ten comprised another James Bond film – *Live and Let Die* – two Broadway musicals (*Jesus Christ Superstar* and *Sound of Music* in reissue), two macho-adventure pictures *(The Getaway* and *Deliverance),* Peter Bogdanovich's *Paper Moon;* and two films that really worried the majors – George Lucas's independent blockbuster *American Graffiti* (which all the studios had rejected until Coppola signed on as the film's nominal producer) and a foreign-made picture, Bernardo Bertolucci's *Last Tango in Paris,* at the time the most sexually explicit film ever to be released by a major American studio.

What made *Last Tango* such a big problem for the studios was not only Bertolucci's reputation as an *auteur* who controlled every aspect of production himself, but that three other X-rated films – *Deep Throat, The Devil and Miss Jones,* and *Behind the Green Door*[54] – would also have appeared in the list of the year's top films if at the time *Variety* had not declined to list hardcore releases alongside so-called legit pictures. The hardcore industry's surprising and to an extent mainstream success (in that all three of these films were screened at "legit" venues in major cities across the country) presented a very difficult problem for the major studios. As far back as 1970, a record bad year in the industry, the trades had begun to ponder whether or not an X rating might be the key to future box office success,[55] and from 1971 through 1973, the studios were forced to watch and wait as the porno trade increased its market share and the U.S. Supreme Court sorted out exactly how much or how little communities had to say about what could be shown on local screens.[56]

The eventual insitution of "community standards" as a way of controlling the hardcore industry significantly helped the mainstream studios reestablish control over the marketplace. But from 1970 to 1973, roughly the years covering the development of both *Godfather* pictures, studio executives spent a lot of time worrying about what they might have to do should the courts suppport a fully open marketplace and what sort of concessions they might have to make not only to this new audience but to powerful *auteurs* who, following Bertolucci's lead, might decide that they too wanted to make more explicit movies.

Within a year of the "community standards" decision, the legit industry recovered in dramatic fashion. In 1974, "legit" box office revenues were the second highest in history. But since *The Godfather Part II* opened at the end of December 1974, its revenues were not recorded until the start of the following year. As a result, 1974 was not a particularly good year for Paramount and it was a particularly bad year for Yablans. In a major industry surprise, on September 25, 1974, two months before the release of *The Godfather Part II,* Gulf & Western CEO Charles Bluhdorn announced that Barry Diller, a thirty-two-year-old television executive at ABC, had been hired to become the new CEO and chairman of the board of Paramount Pictures. Yablans, whom Bluhdorn blamed for the studio's sluggish performance since the release of *The Godfather,* made a quiet exit and Diller was in place in time to lay claim to the box office success of *The Godfather Part II.*[57]

The production of *The Godfather Part II* was significantly less contentious than the production of the first film, largely because Coppola was contracted not only to co-write and direct but to produce the film himself. In the absence of Robert Evans (who was busy producing films under the Paramount-owned Robert Evans Productions banner) and *Godfather* producer Al Ruddy, Coppola seemed to have a free hand, and as a result, the trades had little to report. In fact, the studio seemed to exert its power only once during the development and production of the film, and Coppola quietly acquiesced. After Brando embarrassed the studio by refusing to accept the "Best Actor" Oscar for his performance in *The Godfather* and then audaciously demanded $500,000 plus 10 percent of the gross to appear in the sequel, the studio refused to rehire him.[58] Without Brando, Coppola was forced to alter his original concept for the film. Puzo and Coppola's revised *Godfather II* narrative had a decidedly more elliptical structure than the first film. Unwilling to focus only on Michael Corleone after the move to Nevada, they added a back-story concerning the young Don's navigating the mean streets of New York at the turn of the century. When it came time to produce the picture, Coppola decided to tie the two stories together through a series of dissolves. The two stories aptly characterize organized crime (and its impact on the family) at two very different stages of development, but this theme, and the complex visual and narrative structure that became the hallmark of the film, resulted less from design than from necessity.

The key to Coppola's *Godfather II* contract was the extent of creative autonomy that Yablans was willing, perhaps even anxious, to cede to the director. After the staggering box office grosses earned by *The Godfather* and then *American Graffiti,* Yablans had every reason to believe that Coppola had a better idea of what audiences wanted to see than he did. To his credit, he did not let his ego get in the way of his good judgment; Yablans, after all, was primarily a money (and not a movie) expert.

In addition to an unprecedented freedom from studio interference on the set, Coppola was paid like (indeed, he was treated like) a movie star. He received $250,000 for the script, $200,000 to direct, and, via an absurdly complicated formula, as producer, between 10 and 15 percent of the of the film's net profits which eventually were, as everyone at Paramount had always expected, considerable.[59] (Pacino also did a lot better when he agreed to appear in the sequel; he received $500,000, twenty-five times what he made to play Michael in the first film.)

Coppola brought *The Godfather Part II* in for approximately $15 million, well over twice the production cost of *The Godfather*. But although the studio had hoped to keep the budget in the $8 million range, once the picture was completed there was little cause for concern. *The Godfather Part II* was "off the nut" – it turned a profit – weeks before its first screening, as the studio received over $26 million in exhibitor advances by the first of December 1974.

The Godfather Part II did not break any box office records. It was a hit, but not on the scale of the first film. And to a large extent its success was something of a bad omen, as it revealed a fundamental weakness in the studio's indulgence of the *auteur* theory. Beginning with the rave review in *Variety*, one phrase would continue to haunt executives at Paramount: "Coppola was in total control of Part II."[60]

The film was as successful with the critics as the first picture was successful in the marketplace. Whereas Yablans took out a ten-page ad in *Variety* to herald the record box office figures of *The Godfather,* Diller took out two pages to reprint blurbs from the major reviewers, all of whom raved about *The Godfather Part II*. It was the best and maybe only way to fashion a promotional campaign for the film, but it must have been hard for Diller to accept the notion that when, for once, the studio turned a project over to a director, the result was not only a box office success but, at least according to the critics, one of the two or three best films ever made at a Hollywood studio.

The review by the *New Yorker*'s Pauline Kael seemed to sum up the significance of the picture: "*[The Godfather Part II]* is the work of a major artist, who else, when he got the chance and the power, would have proceeded with the absolute conviction that he'd make the film the way it should be made? In movies, that's the inner voice of an authentic hero."[61] What Kael seemed to acknowledge was not only the film's inherent quality, but its historical significance in terms of a growing American *auteur* tradition. When the film went on to win the Academy Award for "Best Picture" and "Best Director," the studio again dutifully exploited the industry's continued affirmation of the film and its director's apparent brilliance even though doing so seemed to suggest that they were beginning to believe that giving directors carte blanche might actually be a good idea.

Of course, *The Conversation,* a film similarly lauded by the critics, seemed to send another sort of message. Unlike *The Godfather Part II, The Conversation* did little business domestically and seemed to suggest that Coppola might not be kidding about leaving Hollywood to make little independent films on the cheap. However seductive the *auteur* theory seemed at first, by the end of 1974 the studios came to realize how dangerous its implementation could be. After *The Conversation,* studio executives had reason to fear the prospect of more big directors making little, personal films with studio money. And though it hadn't happened yet, an even more perilous scenario loomed: the possibility that someday a director might make a big, personal film.

THE GODFATHER PART III

The Godfather Part III was a project Coppola had steadfastly resisted from 1974 to 1989. He was so against the idea of another sequel that he told the press he would only make a third *Godfather* picture if it could be a farce, like *Abbott and Costello Meet the Godfather.*[62]

Throughout the seventies, the Hollywood rumor was that Paramount wanted to cast John Travolta as the third-generation don, and Coppola would have no part of it. But the truth of the matter is more complicated than that. From 1975 to 1979, Coppola was tied up in the development and production of *Apocalypse Now* and, for the next four years, in an audacious but ill-fated attempt to own his own studio. By 1982, the studio was on the auction block, and two years later, when the lot finally sold, Coppola was contemplating bankruptcy in order to gain protection from debts stemming from the creative financing of the production of *One from the Heart,* a picture that lost in the neighborhood of $27 million.[63]

By 1985, Coppola's reputation had declined so significantly that Paramount executives had begun to think about making the film without him. Rumor has it that Paramount CEO Frank Mancuso actually offered the film to Russian-born director Andrei Konchalovski and then to stars Sylvestor Stallone and Eddie Murphy, but no suitable deal could be struck. In 1989, when Mancuso decided to offer the picture to Coppola again, the director was inclined to accept; he was out of money and he hadn't had a hit in over ten years.[64]

Additionally, Coppola had warmed to the idea because two years earlier, Mancuso had been generous in first financing and then promoting Coppola's semi-autobiographical *Tucker: The Man and His Dream*. When *Tucker* was released in 1988 to disappointing grosses, Mancuso supported it anyway in the press. Perhaps it was the least he could do, and once ancillary monies were factored in, Paramount may have been in the black on the film anyway. But Mancuso's support was a lot more than Coppola had grown accustomed to in the eighties, and it no doubt went a long way toward mending Coppola's relationship with the studio.[65]

It is conceivable that Mancuso cynically used his investment in and cooperation during the production and release of *Tucker* to eventually convince Coppola to direct *The Godfather Part III*. If he did, it was a smart move on his part. By 1989, the first two *Godfather* films had grossed in excess of $800 million. If Mancuso had to lose money on *Tucker* in order to package *The Godfather Part III*, it was money well spent.

Moreover, at the time, Mancuso realized that Paramount needed the film as much as Coppola did. The studio was still reeling from a corporate shake-up that followed the death of Gulf & Western CEO Charles Bluhdorn in 1983. Bluhdorn's successor was the far more fiscally conservative Martin Davis, whose first move as CEO was to put Mancuso, a marketing expert, in charge of the studio. In doing so, he reneged on a deal made by Bluhdorn with the more production-oriented (and less easily controlled) studio chairman Barry Diller, an arrangement that guaranteed the former ABC-TV executive that his autonomy and power at Paramount would increase in time. Diller filed suit for breach of contract – which was settled out of court – and then took a parallel position at Fox.[66]

Soon after Diller announced his decision to leave the studio, his second in command, Michael Eisner, resigned. A few weeks later, Eisner was named CEO at Disney. Then, in a dramatic display of distrust for the new Paramount leadership, Jeffrey Katzenberg, Bill Mechanic, Helene Hahn, Richard Frank, and Bob Jacquemin – top executives in the creative and legal departments – left to join Eisner at Disney. What made the mass resignations all the more embarrassing was that at the time Disney was not a major studio; it had just survived a calamitous buy-out attempt and seemed destined to face another unless Eisner could turn the company around completely.

To Davis's chagrin, by the end of the decade, the Disney turnaround was complete; under Eisner's leadership, the studio was well on its way to becoming the most powerful entertainment conglomerate on the planet. In the meantime, under Davis and Mancuso, Paramount seemed to lack direction. They continued to produce money-making movies – *Top Gun* was the number one and *Crocodile Dundee* the number two film in 1986; *Fatal Attraction* ranked a close second behind Disney's *Three Men and a Baby* the following year – but for the most part the studio's hottest properties were those dating back to previous regimes: the Indiana Jones films, the *Star Trek* series, *Beverly Hills Cop,* and virtually anything else with Eddie Murphy (including the astoundingly bad *Coming to America,* which somehow grossed over $128 million in 1988). Though it was *just* a sequel (in an era of sequels) and very much a film tied to Paramount's recent past, *The Godfather Part III* was also a prestige project, and Paramount needed the film to reestablish its legitimacy as a studio that (also) made quality pictures.

More importantly, by the end of 1989, the Mancuso needed the film to deflect attention away from what emerged as the most significant trade story of the year, a story in which Paramount clearly came out the loser. In April, Gulf & Western announced its decision to sell off its "financial unit" in order to consolidate its interests in the entertainment industry. Less than two months later, Davis took out a full-page advertisement in *Variety* to announce the company's new name: Paramount Communications Inc.[67] Davis's new, diversified studio seemed well set up to do business in the nineties; its holdings crossed genres and industries, and it had the ability to reproduce a single product in various forms (or formats) within a family of companies either owned outright or controlled by Davis. But despite the apparent wisdom of Davis's consolidation of the company's resources, the trades seemed interested only in speculating about what Paramount planned to do with all the cash it netted from the sale and who might make a move on the company if Davis failed to find a place for it soon.

The amount of cash in question was significant by any standards: $3.5 billion. MCA was an announced target (it would eventually go to the Japanese electronics multinational, Matsushita), and then there were rumors regarding the Chicago-based Tribune Corporation (which owned a number of newspapers and television stations – ABC, CBS, NBC and Time Inc.), which at the time had announced its intention to merge with Warner Communications (WCI).[68] Also in the rumor mill was the possibility of a Paramount merger with Sumner Redstone's Viacom, a company that owned theaters, cable television systems, and the cable stations Showtime, The Movie Channel, and MTV.[69]

On June 6, 1989, Davis finally made his move, and it was a shocker; he went after Time. From that date until September 20, 1989, the battle between WCI and Paramount dominated the trades.[70] The story seemed to foreground the stakes and the shape of yet another new Hollywood – one in which, as *Variety*'s Richard Gold so glibly put it, "all of show business [will be] controlled by two or three conglomerates."[71]

Davis had a number of reasons for launching the hostile $10.7 billion, $175 per share offer for Time: (1) the deal promised to give Paramount a productive place to put its excess cash to work, (2) given Time and Paramount's extensive holdings in publishing, the combined companies could nearly monopolize the print market, and (3) Davis's offer and subsequent legal challenge to the Time-

WCI merger clearly unnerved his long-time nemesis, Steve Ross, and the rest of the team at WCI at the precise moment that the Warner Brothers film studio was riding high, sporting dazzling box office numbers with *Batman,* a film that eventually earned over $250 million domestically.

The Paramount–WCI battle is too involved and too confusing to get into any deeper here; in the end, a Delaware Supreme Court judge quashed Paramount's attempt to challenge the deal, and eventually Time simplified things by acquiring WCI outright. By the time the Time/Life deal was closed, Paramount had more to worry about than the good fortune of one of its competitors. Speculation resumed regarding who might make a move on the studio. Likely suitors included Telecommunications, Inc. (TCI), Cablevision Systems, NBC's parent General Electric, Sony, Bertelsmann of West Germany, and Hachette of France.[72] It is an irony no doubt lost on the players involved, but at the very moment Coppola was preparing a script about Machiavellian players involved in international superdeals, Paramount found itself involved in a discomfortingly similar scenario.

The production of *The Godfather Part III* went relatively smoothly because both Mancuso and Coppola needed a hit and neither could afford to push the other around. The most significant problem faced by Coppola was Mancuso's single-minded focus on getting the film out in time for Christmas 1990; he was, after all, a marketing not a production executive. When Mancuso signed Coppola to write and direct the picture, Coppola asked for six months to develop a story and script. Mancuso gave him six weeks. To Mancuso's credit, he understood that it was Coppola's job to make sure that *The Godfather Part III* looked like an event film, but it was up to him to see that it got into the right theaters during the peak season.

Mancuso's original budget for *The Godfather Part III* was $44 million, somewhat steep at the time, even for such a big picture. One reason for the film's cost was its exorbitant above-the-line salaries. Mancuso agreed to pay Coppola $3 million to direct, $1 million to write, and (according to estimates) as much as another $2 million plus 15 percent of the gross to produce the film. In order to get the production phase under way as quickly as possible, Mancuso met Al Pacino's asking price of $5 million and Diane Keaton's for $2 million.

But then, mysteriously, Mancuso balked at paying Robert Duvall more than $1.5 million.[73] Duvall walked and as a result Coppola had to rewrite the script, excising a main character, Michael's attorney and adopted brother Tom. In his place, Coppola introduced a new character, a slick WASP lawyer (played by George Hamilton). Mancuso's refusal to meet Duvall's asking price had a significant impact on the film; it further disconnected *The Godfather Part III* from its two predecessors, it seemed to strengthen the film's thematic attending legitimacy as a betrayal of family and ethnicity, and it ultimately altered the way many people read the film (in that Hamilton's presence served as a reminder of Duvall's absence).

Eventually, a second casting problem emerged. Winona Ryder, contracted to play Mary, Michael's daughter, arrived on the set exhausted and had to be sent home. Coppola decided to replace her with his "real-life" daughter Sofia, who had virtually no acting experience. Mancuso countered with an offer to hire any Hollywood actress – even, it was rumored at the time, Madonna (who had screen-tested for the role months earlier but was rejected because she was too old for the part). Coppola shrewdly argued that casting someone else would put the film behind schedule and Mancuso gave in.

Despite all the pressure from Mancuso, Coppola completed the shoot behind schedule. Again, in order to get the film in theaters in time for Christmas, Mancuso hired a virtual army of editors, had them work around the clock, and paid (all told) approximately fifty times what it would have cost to hire a single editor to cut and mix the film. As with so many "event pictures" in the new Hollywood, once the film got under way, money, in staggering amounts, was always available.

As Mancuso had hoped, *The Godfather Part III* was released in time for Christmas 1990. It cost approximately $54 million to produce, about $10 million more than he had originally budgeted for the film. To a large extent, the overage was Mancuso's fault and to his credit, even when the film did not hit as big as he had hoped, he never publically blamed Coppola for failing to keep to the budget.[74] He understood that *his* rush to get the film out in time for the holidays was the "real" reason for the budget overage, and he no doubt realized that the film's initial domestic box office was just a very small part of its larger significance to the studio.

In its initial domestic release, *The Godfather Part III* grossed approximately $70 million; taken on its own, a disappointingly low figure. Adjusting for the change in the value of 1972, 1974, and 1990 dollars and the difference in ticket prices, *The Godfather Part III* was, by a significant margin, the least successful of the three *Godfather* films. But in Hollywood, these days, theatrical box office is a very small part of a film's worth to a studio. In addition to the domestic theatrical release of *The Godfather Part III*, the studio controlled the picture's videocassette and pay-television rights and also stood to benefit from the foreign distribution of the film. In Europe, where Coppola's reputation has never flagged as it has here, *The Godfather Part III* promised to be major event.

Paramount further protected itself by piggybacking the simultaneous re-release of the first two *Godfather* pictures in a special videocassette box set, featuring, as has become a fashionable industry practice, "footage never before seen" edited back into a so-called director's cut.[75] The studio also coordinated a rescreening of the first two *Godfather* films on (Time-Warner's) HBO, which not only produced revenue for the studio but helped turn the release of *The Godfather Part III* into a multimedia event.

Even more importantly, Paramount's stake in the picture had no time limit. The studio could (and did) take its time releasing *The Godfather Part III* to cable and to video rental and sales outlets. Moreover, as Mancuso had hoped it would, the film proved that Paramount was (once again) capable of making a prestige picture. Just two months after its nationwide release, *The Godfather Part III* received Academy Award nominations for "Best Picture," "Best Director," and "Best Actor."[76]

Throughout the production, Coppola had to deal with a series of setbacks in his attempt to secure bankruptcy protection from debts dating back to 1982. On January 25, 1990, Coppola listed liabilities amounting to $28.9 million. A lot of the money was (still) owed to Jack Singer, a Canadian financier who had loaned Coppola $3 million in 1981 to help finance the production of *One from the Heart*. In 1984, Singer ended up purchasing Coppola's studio (from Security Pacific Bank, which eventually foreclosed on the property), but continued to view the $3 million as a separate production loan. By 1990, at 18 percent interest, Singer claimed that Coppola owed him in excess of $7 million.

Coppola discussed the relevance of the bankruptcy proceedings to the production of *The Godfather Part III* in a 1992 interview felicitously but aptly titled "Will [Coppola's] new film, *Bram Stoker's Dracula*, drive a stake into his credibility, or resurrect his creative might?" Asked about his state of mind while working on *The Godfather Part III*, Coppola responded: ". . . at that point I was being sued and pursued by the man who got my studio, and he wanted another $7 million. So I just made *Godfather III* the way I felt about things and, in a way, put myself in Michael Corleone's shoes."[77]

There was an ironic back-story to Coppola's battle with Singer in that Coppola's legal strategy to cancel the debt depended on largely unsubstantiated accusations connecting Singer to organized crime. In 1989, Coppola's lawyers contended that the original $3 million Singer loaned Coppola was money the Canadian millionaire had earned from illegal racketeering activities in Texas and thus was not subject to repayment. A California court saw things differently.

At the very moment he seemed on the verge of something of a comeback in Hollywood, Coppola had to post a $12 million bond in order to hold onto his house and his Napa Valley vineyard. And though he stood to receive over $6 million for his work on *The Godfather Part III*, it was unclear at the time who exactly would get to enjoy all that money.[78]

Approximately two weeks after the premiere of *The Godfather*

Part III, former Paramount executive Peter Bart introduced a second gangland subtext. In a page one article titled "How Par[amount] Wised up to Wiseguys on the Backlot," Bart contended that, in 1972, "interests closely linked to the mob had managed to establish a secret beachhead at Paramount," and moreover, that they did so as the result of a significant investment in the studio made by a notorious Sicilian financier named Michele Sindona. In the early seventies, Sindona entered into a complex deal with then Gulf & Western chairman Charles Bluhdorn, one that was central to the dramatic turnaround at Paramount at the very moment Evans, Coppola, and Puzo were developing *The Godfather*. Bluhdorn helped Sindona purchase a 20 percent share in a Vatican-held company, the Societa General Immobiliare. Immobiliare, in turn, purchased a significant interest in Paramount, providing the studio with much-needed capital.

Rumors of Sindona's mob connections – that he was the Gambino family's financial adviser – began to circulate only after his arrest and conviction for fraud and his subsequent extradition to Italy to stand trial for murder (where, in 1986, he died in jail under mysterious circumstances).

According to Bart, in an effort to convince Coppola to make a third *Godfather* film in the early eighties, Bluhdorn told Coppola what he knew about Sindona, about his deal with the Vatican and how the mysterious death of the so-called Smiling Pope, John Paul I, perhaps stemmed from it. In *The Godfather Part III*, it is Michael Corleone who attempts to buy a controlling interest in the shadowy conglomerate, Immobiliare, and then loses his advantage when a pope is assasinated after little more than a month in office. It is in acknowledgment of his meeting with Bluhdorn and the various connections between the executive's story and the one told in *The Godfather Part III*, Bart contends, that Coppola ultimately decided to dedicate the film to Bluhdorn's memory.[79]

Looking back, it is hard to miss the irony in Bart's story; ultimately, it was a secret investment by a reputed Sicilian gangster that made possible the production of maybe the best gangster film ever made. That the film played such a large part in the industry turnaround in the early seventies seems to suggest that Sindona's investment dramatically changed the fortunes not only of the studio but perhaps of all of Hollywood as well.

NOTES

1. Dave Kaufman, "Hollywood Unemployment at 42.8%," *Variety* (March 4, 1970), 3.
2. Thomas Pryor, "Hollywood Future Riding on Box Office," *Variety* (July 1, 1970), 1.
3. "Majors' 1971 Rentals Projection," *Variety* (November 29, 1972), 5.
4. "Paramount Studio Buy Talks, But No Deal Yet into Focus; Realty Value Runs $29–32-Mil," *Variety* (April 8, 1970), 5.
5. During the production of *The Godfather*, Yablans blamed the New York unions for upping the location production budget by $10,000 a day. See Abel Green, "Yablans Raps Union Costs," *Variety* (September 8, 1971), 5.
6. "Cinema Intl. Cuts Par-U Fee," *Variety* (May 27, 1970), 3.
7. Gene Arnell, "Yablans into Paramount Presidency; He and Jafe on Ideal Budgets," *Variety* (May 5, 1971), 3.
8. At the time, Paramount owned the Famous Players theater chain in Canada but could not control the exhibition of their own product in the United States. Today, of course, not only can virtually all the studios control the exhibition of their product, Paramount is (at this writing) owned by Viacom and its partner Blockbuster Video – the first a cable television operator, the second a videocassette retailer – both in the business of exhibiting motion pictures. In its purchase of Cap Cities/ABC, Disney has acquired an additional television outset for its product and an alternative means for packaging its product (with Cap Cities ESPN) to cable television venues overseas.
9. As cited in Robert Evans, *The Kid Stays in the Picture* (New York: Hyperion, 1994), 114.
10. Peter Bart in the Introduction to Evans, *The Kid Stays in the Picture*, xiv.
11. Evans, *The Kid Stays in the Picture*, 182.
12. Peter Cowie, "The Whole Godfather," *Connoisseur* (December 1990), 90. Cowie is also the author of *Coppola* (New York: Scribners, 1990).
13. Cowie, "The Whole Godfather," 90.
14. These are the directors listed by Evans in *The Kid Stays in the Picture*, 218.
15. These are the names added to Evans's list by Cowie in "The Whole Godfather," 90.
16. Evans, *The Kid Stays in the Picture*, 220.

17. Ibid.
18. It is Evans who characterizes Korshak as a mob lawyer. Evans, *The Kid Stays in the Picture*, 4, 222–224.
19. Evans, *The Kid Stays in the Picture*, 223–224.
20. "Brando's Mute Test Copped Role; *Godfather* Funnier Than Mafia Picnic," *Variety* (March 8, 1972), 6; and "Godfather May Top GWTW [*Gone with the Wind*]," *Variety* (March 8, 1972), 254. Rumor has it that Brando's agent either squandered or legitimately sold off Brando's cut; as with so much contemporary Hollywood history, it is difficult to simply follow the money.
21. For more on the Evans–Coppola feud, see Jon Lewis, *Whom God Wishes to Destroy . . . Francis Coppola and the New Hollywood* (Durham, NC: Duke University Press, 1995), 111–113, 119–121, 123–138.
22. William Murry, "*Playboy* Interview: Francis Ford Coppola," *Playboy* 22 (1975), 59.
23. David Thomson and Lucy Gray, "Idols of the King," *Film Comment* (September–October 1983), 72–73.
24. Julie Saloman, "Budget Busters: *The Cotton Club*'s Battle of the Bulge," *Wall Street Journal* (December 13, 1984), 22.
25. Evans, *The Kid Stays in the Picture*, 343.
26. Ibid., 344.
27. Peter Bart in the Foreword to Ibid., xiv.
28. Evans, *The Kid Stays in the Picture*, 225. Evans tells this story to show that he never really had anything against Coppola personally, that he in fact protected Coppola against various behind-the-scenes plots to get him fired off the film.
29. Cowie, "The Whole Godfather," 92. Of course, Brando would have had every reason to favor Kazan over Coppola; after all, Kazan had directed Brando in *On the Waterfront* and *A Streetcar Named Desire*. That he supported Coppola through this crisis must have boosted Coppola's confidence, which was continually under siege during the production, so much so that Gulf & Western CEO Charles Bluhdorn became a regular visitor to the set, presumably to prevent any additional behind-the-scenes maneuvering from disrupting or delaying the production of the picture. According to all acounts I've read, Bluhdorn's presence on the set never seemed to worry Coppola; instead, the two became friends.
30. Gene Arneel, "Cut Directors Down to Size: Bob Evans: 'We Keep Control,'" *Variety* (February 3, 1971), 1, 22.
31. "Evans May Have Been Thinking of Her," *Variety* (February 10, 1971).
32. Lee Beaupre, "Deflate 'Big Me' Directors: Film Producers See a Credit Gap," *Variety* (May 2, 1973). Note that even after the release of *The Godfather*, Evans continued to use the trades to reassert studio control over the product.

33. Grace Lichtenstein, "'Godfather' Film Won't Mention Mafia," *New York Times* (March 20, 1971), 1, 34.
34. Fred Ferretti, "Corporate Rift in 'Godfather' Filming," *New York Times* (March 23, 1971), 28.
35. "Yes Mr. Ruddy, There Is a . . . ," (editorial), *New York Times* (March 23, 1971), 36.
36. "Damone Drops Role in 'Godfather' Film," *New York Times* (April 5, 1971), 31.
37. "Par Repudiates Italo-Am. Group vs. 'Godfather,'" *Variety* (March 24, 1971). Note that the piece was published the day after the *New York Times* editorial. (See note 35.)
38. In order to secure an exclusive showing of *The Godfather*, exhibitors were asked to advance a fee (as a guarantee against box office receipts). By March 15, these cash advances had exceeded $15 million. Once the film was in general release, Paramount received a 90/10 spilt – they received 90 percent of the gate after theater expenses – at all of the 340 venues scheduled to show the film nationwide.
39. Advertisement in *Variety* (March 29, 1972), 7–16. This strategy was used only once before in recent memory at Paramount, predictably attending the release of *Love Story*. See *Variety* (January 18, 1971), 10–12.
40. Advertisement in *Variety* (April 12, 1972), 10–11.
41. See "Loews' National Share 'Godfather' on Its L.A. Start," *Variety* (February 16, 1972), 4; and "1970–'71–'72 Pacers," *Variety* (July 26, 1972), 5.
42. See "'Godfather' of All; Includes Wall Street," *Variety* (April 12, 1972), 4; and A. D. Murphy, "'Godfather' and Other Goodies," *Variety* (November 15, 1972), 3.
43. Coppola, though, lost to Bob Fosse and *Cabaret* for "Best Director," one of the rare times the "Best Picture" and "Best Director" awards were split and one of the even rarer times the winner of the Directors' Guild Award (Coppola) lost on Oscar night. That said, Coppola did not exit the 1972 awards empty-handed, winning a share of the "Best Screenplay" and (as one of the film's producers) "Best Picture" Oscars.
44. The year-end box office figures printed in *Variety* appeared under an ominous headline: "'Godfather' & Rest." See *Variety* (January 3, 1973), 7.
45. I provide a similar discussion of the Directors Company in context to Coppola's ambitions early on his career in Lewis, *Whom God Wishes to Destroy*, 16–18.
46. Frank Yablans, "Bold Approach to Pix B.O.; and TV's Production Virility Yet to Be Tested," *Variety* (January 3, 1973), 24.
47. Michael Pye and Lynda Myles, *The Movie Brats* (New York: Holt, 1975), 97.

48. Ibid.
49. "Friedkin Exits Directors Co.," *Variety* (September 11, 1974), 3.
50. Richard Albarino, "Coppola's Plans: To Lay Low in Frisco, Little Pic Project," *Variety* (March 27, 1974), 6.
51. "Coppola's Cozy Rugoff Deal," *Variety* (January 22, 1975), 5, 90.
52. "Cinema 5 Quarter Net 60G; Cause Mostly Swedish Import; Coppola at Annual meeting," *Variety* (January 29, 1975), 3. All three films eventually made it to the screen, though none of them were released by Coppola through Cinema 5.
53. Though the studio's box office revenues were off for the year, Paramount produced a number of interesting movies: the modest box office hit *The Great Gatsby, Mikey and Nicky, The Parallax View,* and *Serpico.* Actually, Yablans had good reason to blame himself for the studio's declining revenue share, having sold off 50 percent of the studio's stake in the box office hit *Lady Sings the Blues* to Berry Gordy when the film went over budget.
54. See "Throat Profits versus Non-Porno Field," *Variety* (July 4, 1973); and "1973: Moments of Truth for Film," *Variety* (January 9, 1974), 44.
55. See "Trade Ponders: X the Key to B.O.," *Variety* (February 25, 1970), 1.
56. See Gene Arneel, "Puts Class in Bed with Porno," *Variety* (May 6, 1970); "Recent Supreme Court Rulings Tending to Set Limits on Porno; Rebuff of Idea of Anything Goes," *Variety* (May 12, 1971); Theodore Kupferman, "Obscenity Law Can't Keep Changing,"*Variety* (January 5, 1972); "Show Biz's Fig-Leaf Crisis: High Court Hands Reins over Porno to Local Judges," *Variety* (June 27, 1973), 1, 78; and Addison Verril, "Community Standards Spells C-O-N-F-U-S-I-O-N," *Variety* (June 27, 1973), 5.
57. A. D. Murphy, "Barry Diller, 32, New Par Chairman: Bluhdorn Move Surprises Film Trade," *Variety* (September 25, 1974).
58. "Brando Makes Demands, Can Paramount Refuse?" *Variety* (November 19, 1972), 3.
59. "'Godfather' Ups Pacino, Coppola to Stratosphere," *Variety* (August 15, 1973), 1.
60. "The Godfather Part II" (review), *Variety* (December 11, 1974).
61. Pauline Kael, "The Curent Cinema" (review of *The Godfather Part II*), *New Yorker* (December 23, 1974), 63–68.
62. Jack Kroll, "The Corleones' Return," *Newsweek* (December 24, 1990), 58.
63. The Zoetrope Studios "project" is long story, one I tell in *Whom God Wishes to Destroy.*
64. *Only two of Coppola's films in the 1980s turned a profit:* The Outsiders, a film produced with the sole intention of paying the bills at Zoetrope Studios, and *Peggy Sue Got Married,* a film he did not write, develop, or produce.
65. In 1982, then Paramount chairman Barry Diller reneged on an

agreement to distribute *One from the Heart* and in doing so bankrupted Coppola and his studio. That Coppola was willing to believe that he actually owed Paramount a favor after the release of *Tucker: The Man and His Dream* only six years later supports the old industry adage that it pays to have a short memory.

66. Since his exit from Fox, Diller has remained in the news, recently vying for control of his old studio (with backing from cable television millionaire John Malone). Diller lost out to Sumner Redstone and Viacom and has since failed in attempts to take over CBS and to become the CEO of post–Matsushita MCA.

67. *Variety* (June 7–13, 1989), 15.

68. Richard Gold, "G&W Pares Down to Media Only; Possibilities Abound," *Variety* (April 12–18, 1989), 1, 4.

69. "Pending Sale of Associates First Indicates G&W May Be Considering Viacom Merger," *Variety* (May 10–18, 1989), 3.

70. See Richard Gold, "Size Is the Ultimate Prize as Showbiz/Media Corps Fight for Supremacy," *Variety* (June 14–20, 1989), 1, 6; Richard Gold, "Will Par-Time-WCI War Victimize Creatives," *Variety* (June 21–27, 1989), 1, 4; Richard Gold, "Intense Propoganda Fight Marks Par vs. WCI War, *Variety* (June 26–July 4, 1989), 1, 5; Richard Gold, "Par's Block Looks Like a Bust as Court Backs Time Director's Stand," *Variety* (July 19–25, 1989), 1, 6; Richard Gold and Paul Harris, "Time Marches on, Grabs Warner, Outpaces Par," *Variety* (July 26–August 1, 1989), 1, 6; "Time Inc. Buyout Attempt Puts Dent in Paramount Communications Qtr.," *Variety* (September 20–26, 1989), 9.

71. Richard Gold, "Size Is the Ultimate Prize," 1.

72. Richard Gold, "Paramount Should Look to Buy Elsewhere, Lest It Be Taken Over Itself, Experts Say," *Variety* (July 19–25, 1989), 6.

73. Kroll, "The Corleones' Return," 58–61. See also Jack Kroll, "The Offer He Didn't Refuse, *Newsweek* (May 28, 1990), 68–69.

74. Kroll, "The Corleone's Return," 58.

75. This "director's cut" was actually "cut" by longtime Coppola editor Barry Malkin and closely resembled *The Godfather Saga,* which aired on network television following the release of *The Godfather Part II.*

76. I also discuss *The Godfather Part III* in *Whom God Wishes to Destroy,* 154–159.

77. Graham Fuller, "Francis Ford Coppola: "Will His New Film, *Bram Stoker's Dracula,* Drive a Stake into His Credibility, or Resurrect His Creative Might?" *Interview* (November, 1992), 117.

78. See: Richard Gold, "Coppola Bankruptcy Baffles Creditors and Colleagues," *Variety* (January 31, 1990), 1, 4; and Peter Hlavacek, "Apocalypse Now, Chapter Eleven," *Variety* (March 14, 1990), 3, 14.

79. Peter Bart, "How Par Wised Up to Wiseguys on Backlot," *Variety* (January 7, 1991), 1, 110.

2 *The Godfather* and the Mythology of Mafia

What we call Mafia is a most peculiar organization. It is a secret society that is, in fact, so secret that it denies its own existence. The traditional code of the mafioso (which has been broken by many in the last decade, as is discussed later) prescribes that once arrested, one should deny any association with or knowledge of the organization, to the extent of dismissing the very notion of Mafia as "a myth." However, the Mafia is also a powerful apparatus of symbolic production, deeply concerned with its own appearance. The language, the rituals, the means of communication to the enemy, the overarching value system are well thought out and handed down among the mafiosi with particular pride and care. In other words, the "myth" is not left to the imagination of the media and the public; on the contrary, it is created, preserved, and presented by the Mafia itself. Like a religious sect rather than a political movement or a straightforward criminal enterprise, the Mafia has defined its own identity in terms of myth; it has "chosen" and endeavored to become a myth.

The Godfather is the broadest representation of this myth in our days; it made it into a popular culture staple with worldwide appeal. What I am concerned with here is the process by which a self-generated, culturally specific myth is translated into the language of popular culture and made into a hugely successful product. The question has at least three ramifications: what does this "translation" do to the myth, what does it do to the myth's subject (the Mafia), and what does it do to our culture?

We need to start this discussion with an attempt to characterize more specifically what the myth of the Mafia consists of. There is an inherent danger in this attempt, because the myth is so shrouded in mystery and ambiguity. One could easily extract from Mafia culture a simple, consistent, user-friendly manual. But that would be missing the point that mystery and ambiguity are not just the function of security from the law and of the discrepancy between self-perception and outside perception. Rather, they are there by design, they are part of this myth's genetic makeup.

Mystery: The Mafia doesn't publish its statute or its objectives, it doesn't necessarily take claim for its actions, it avoids written records, it questions the very usefulness of verbal communication. Nobody knows for sure when, how, or even why the organization was started. Nobody has provided any conclusive evidence as to what the name itself means. Some believe it stands for "Morte Alla Francia Italia Anela" (Italy wishes death to France) or "Mazzini Autorizza Furti Incendi Avvelenamenti" (Mazzini authorizes thefts, arsons, and poisonings). Others believe that it comes from the words *Ma Fija* (My daughter), which a mother screamed endlessly after her daughter was killed by foreign soldiers, until those words became a whole town's battle cry. Interestingly, these are all expressions of Italian patriotism, although the emphasis is respectively on revenge, lawlessness, mourning. But most serious scholars, in fact, agree by now that Mafia is not an acronym or an exclamation. Most likely, it is a derivate of the word *mafioso,* which indicates a combination of beauty and pride. Although the variety of theories about the name is a good measure of the latitude covered by the Mafia's cultural reach, the interesting paradox is that this reach extends itself "by default," by virtue of its very resistance to a specific definition.

Ambiguity: As many a Mafia observer would say, "nothing is Mafia and everything is Mafia." There is no activity, no area of society that is inherently the Mafia's concern, but they all *can* be. There is no easy way to set the Mafia apart from the general culture it operates within. The diffidence toward verbalization that I referred to earlier, for instance, is a distinctive trait of the Sicilian mentality at large. (Consider the proverb *"A cchiu' bedda parola e' chidda ca 'un si dice,"* or: the most beautiful word is the one you don't say). In many respects, the Mafia phenomenon stems from, mimics, and heightens the Sicilian mentality – and in a larger sense, within American culture, the Italian. At the same time that it rapes and pillages a land and a population, the Mafia has always claimed to protect them and always evinced a sense of belonging. (Conversely, although this land and this population have voiced their suffering, they have also given the Mafia refuge, implicit understanding, patience, and even an odd form of respect.) At the same time that it makes an industry of crime and violence, the Mafia claims to support Christian values and the Catholic church. The ritual by which new members are inducted into a Mafia family is a pseudo-religious ceremony that combines icons of sainthood with what is basically a vote of commitment to violence.

The double morality of the mafioso – absolute ruthlessness against his enemies, but absolute devotion to his family and friends – is in fact a radical schism that informs the overall myth to such a degree that it could be seen as its very core. In other words, the ability to function from one level to the other – from murder to family, from extinguishing life to protecting it – and even more specifically, to do one *because* of the other, could be the quintessential credo of the Mafia myth. The real credo, of course, is making money; but it would be simplistic to deny the Mafia any sincerity. The myth would have no power if its messengers didn't buy into it.

The mythical mafioso, therefore, is a mysterious man and a man of contradictions. He associates with other men in secret, to conduct a business that is vastly unaccountable and in constant mutation. He is a living conspiracy, whose ideal methods of communication are so minimalistic that a nuance of expression should be able to settle matters of life and death. He goes to church, and raises his children within religious traditions; yet his conscience isn't troubled by the responsibility of taking lives. He is a caring, conservative family man who abhors domestic abuse, adultery, and drug use, while he makes his living by abusing the next guy or selling him "vice." This dichotomy is the crux of the mafioso's identity: he must be able to connect these two polarities, to hold them together as if they were meant to fit. It is a sign of his strength to recompose such contradictions within the appearance of a coherent personal whole. The permanent "spiritual exercise" to contain the tension, to avoid a complete personality split without letting one aspect overrule the other – getting soft with the enemies, or getting hard with friends – is the great life lesson of which the mafioso considers himself the keeper.

The concept of family is most important to the mafioso, because it is the one that must come first, the one that provides justification and comfort. In *The Godfather* saga, Don Corleone is, first and foremost, a family man. The mutual loyalty of fathers and sons is the emotional core of the story: fathers "do what they have to do" to grant their sons a better life; sons inherit the mantle to defend the achievements and the honor of their fathers. The affirmation of this bond is the ultimate value; profit and power are just means to an end. This fact is overlooked by the many critics who consider the film a metaphor for capitalist business. Capitalist morality is individualistic; every man can and should make his own success, while society at large benefits from this competition and regulates it for maximum efficiency. But a mafioso who works for himself is a theoretical impossibility, a flagrant violation of the organization's ethics. He needs a family to provide for, children to carry his name. The whole group of fellow mafiosi he is associated with is also called "a family," whose collective interest is inseparable from that of the individuals. This is an ideology of the proletariat or of the aristocracy. It is not as deeply ingrained in the bourgeoisie. A proletarian is somebody whose only richness is in his progeny; an aristocrat is somebody whose richness lies in his name. Reproduction, not production, is in both cases the key to "success": the fact of having children, or the very fact of having been the child of the right parents. For the bourgeoisie, the individual achievements and transient properties are what matters; things material but impermanent define his place in the world.

From a socioeconomic standpoint, the Mafia represents in fact

a confluence of aristocratic and proletarian interests. The organization flourished in Sicily, which was at the time a distinctly non-
industrialized, precapitalist area where the economy (and the
social struggle) revolved around the land. The Mafia's first large-
scale business was the protection of the Sicilian latifundio, the
vast landed estates that the local farmers worked but couldn't
claim. Members of the dispossessed class were recruited by the
landowners to protect by means of prevarication an antiquated
status quo. The Mafia's attachment to its geographical origins is
therefore not just cultural, but economical: belonging to/owning
the land is the original form of its identity. And owning the land,
rather than owning stock or commercial concerns, is what drives
both the peasant and the aristocrat. So, on one hand the Mafia
has come into existence to perpetuate a historically obsolete privilege. On the other hand, like most forms of organized crime, it has
given the underprivileged a way to short-circuit the dynamics of
social rise. By virtue of its self-conferred authority, it has expedited
the transition from proletarian to the modern equivalent of an
aristocrat – the kind that doesn't need a title to advertise the status
of non-work-related privilege. The intermediate level of orderly
competition in the marketplace is skipped, or burned through.
This shouldn't be mistaken for a revolutionary political agenda:
the Mafia doesn't believe in *changing* the system, but in *beating* it.
From a political standpoint, it is inherently conservative: its roots
are in the employ of the landowners, its friends are among the
repositories of power. The Mafia's efforts at self-legitimization have
always been about tradition, its sensibility always nostalgic.

   We are touching here on another interesting paradox of the
Mafia psychology: velocity (in the acquisition of status) and permanence (of the underpinning values) as twin engines – looking
ahead with predatory appetite, while always looking back. But the
side of permanence is the most important one. The Mafia distinguishes itself from any kind of economic, political, or even criminal organization because it transcends its own goals, it withstands
failure, and it tends to reproduce itself for the tautological reason
that it is built along generational lines. Ultimately, the Mafia's

"family values" are key to its power. The Mafia must believe itself to be about "fathers and sons," because this makes it impervious to the blows of the enemy. And ultimately, it must believe that the past was always better, no matter how poor, because only a veneration for the past provides identity and strength in the present.

There is a twisted heroism in this weltanschauung. Living in poverty, contrary to the obvious projection of greed, is a major virtue according to the Mafia myth. The mythical mafioso (or the mafioso as he wants to be seen) shuns the most apparent accoutrements of richness in favor of a simple, self-content family life and nonperishable properties. He can endure the sacrifices of being on the lam or even being in prison, because he never lost the familiarity with deprivation, and because he does it all for the family – not for himself. This self-image has served the mafioso well until recent years. Every professional criminal knows the importance of being able to endure incarceration: "If you can't do the time, don't do the crime." For a criminal organization such as the Mafia, endurance is even more important because of the vast potential damage associated with defection. This is why going to prison has traditionally been considered an essential rite of passage, a baptism by fire that proves the worth of a man. (The organization does everything possible to make life in prison less hard for its members, but ultimately they are supposed to take what's coming to them without complaint.) In a broader sense, the vital necessity of a code of silence explains why the overall "moral standards" of the Mafia need to be "higher." When Toto Riina, "capo di tutti i capi" in the Sicilian Cosa Nostra, was arrested in 1993 and confronted in a courtroom his former colleague turned collaborator to the prosecution Tommaso Buscetta, he refused to assess any specific accusation. Buscetta, a man who is considered the most important defector from La Cosa Nostra and was punished for it with the extermination of his sons and relatives, is also a man known for having had many women. Sitting next to him in that courtroom in Palermo, Riina – the man responsible for those homicides and a few thousand more, but who always claimed to be just a peasant – refused to "lower himself" to a discussion with such "a nonserious person." The message Riina was sending to the judge was that Buscetta betrayed La Cosa Nostra not because he saw the light, but for the same reasons he betrayed his women – because of a character flaw that made him an undignified, unreliable witness. The larger implication of the message was addressed to Riina's fellow mafiosi: stay pure, stay with one woman, fall back to the way of the ancestors in this time of hardship.

It is worth noting that, conversely, Buscetta himself never saw himself as a traitor. On the contrary, he accused Riina and the Corleonese faction, which had risen to complete hegemony within La Cosa Nostra, of betraying the original Mafia values, such as the protection of women and children against the cycle of revenge. It wasn't he, Buscetta, who had exited the organization, but the organization that had exited the honorable path. Buscetta is a flamboyant and sophisticated raconteur, fond of dishing out properly embellished anecdotes such as his own murder of a Mafia traitor. Knowing that he had been made a target for retribution, this traitor would rarely leave the house, and when he did, he would keep his infant son clutched to his chest. Buscetta would watch him in frustration, loath to take the risk of hurting the baby. Several years later, when the child was old enough to walk and managed to sneak away during a stroll, Buscetta, who had waited patiently all that time, shot the man dead. Although it might be hard for us to find much ethical merit in the action of one who kills a man in front of his son, the anecdote has certainly been made public with the intent of highlighting a "civilization of violence" that is worth regretting. Once women and children are fair game, as they have been for the last two decades, there can be no moral standard left. The past was better.

We can see by now how the mythical mafioso is indeed a sort of hero, a paradigm of masculinity and power balanced by fairness, virtue, and control. He provides a role model that cuts through generations, and a built-in dramatic appeal. In the landscape of popular culture, he is a relative of any battle-scarred soldier, any benign but unyielding ruler, any fearless gunfighter. The differences are obvious, but the point is that this particular charac-

ter finds his place within the spectrum of positive objects of identification for the mass audience (albeit toward the outer rim). Popular culture has had a clear option to cast the mafioso as the
heavy or as a noble and romantic figure, and has often enough
chosen the second way.

Interestingly, the Mafia began to recognize itself with the help
of a series of plays and books, the local equivalent of dime novels,
that celebrated the virtues of this character. The word *mafioso*
became common, the attitude that came with it was imprinted in
the public consciousness. "Mafioso," as we pointed out, comes
before "Mafia": the attitude precedes and founds the organization,
rather than the other way around. Once the original mafiosi
looked into that mirror and liked what they saw, the myth was
born. Fueled by it, the organization began to evolve from a tenta-
tive, spontaneous, and modestly ambitious affair to what is
arguably the most powerful form of organized crime in history.
Public representation through the popular arts has been crucial to
the Mafia self-awareness ever since those days.

In Italy, where explicit political stances in works of art and
entertainment are welcome, and often required, the attitude
toward the Mafia went from the naive fascination of melodrama
to the outrage of social realism. Finally, it achieved an ideal combination of both in the endlessly successful TV series, *La Piovra*
(The Octopus), which has been the most important product of fiction in Italian television since it started in the late 1980s, imagine
a politically correct soap opera about the Mafia and its opponents,
with scarce artistic ambition but with a snappy pechant for drawing from the headlines. As the Mafia couldn't admire itself in the
malevolent semblance portrayed by the heirs of neo-realism (Rosi
to begin with), a sort of media-shy retreat into its conspirational
roots became the prevailing posture during that middle-age
period. By the time *La Piovra* came about, *The Godfather* had
already removed any need for such "shyness."

In the United States, popular culture at first treated the mafioso
as the most common ethnic variation of the gangster, a figure that
came to represent uninhibited, exhilarating wish fulfillment with-

out regard for social constraints – but that for this very reason had to be placed in a battle of good and evil where evil always got punished at the end. This was the framework that the film industry in particular had to adopt, by virtue of the Hays Code. But the breakdown of the Code in the sixties came to herald films of higher moral complexity. It was an environment ready to accommodate *The Godfather*. Finally, this was a major film that unabashedly chose to embrace the Mafia myth and portray the protagonist as a fascinating, multilayered hero.

The Godfather shows a profound understanding of Mafia ethics. Michael Corleone loves his family wholeheartedly and would never dream of neglecting it. He became rich, but doesn't crave luxury. He has preserved the living memory of his father's hardships. The film itself (when we consider the trilogy as a whole) is constructed as a memory, a celebration of the past, effectively amplifying Michael's existential orientation. What makes Michael such a strong, compelling hero and the natural leader of the organization is the requisite ability to kill without blinking because of his love for the family. One of the most unforgettable moments in Coppola's opus is an illustration of this ability: the montage of Michael's enemies being dispatched and his son being baptized. As Carlos Clarens points out in his book *Crime Films*, it's a montage "by opposition" a la Eisenstein, a complex interpolation of conflicting images in which the conflict itself produces meaning (Michael's and Kay's hands undoing the baby's bonnet, a killer's hands gripping his pistol, those of a priest drawing holy water, again a killer's hands extracting his weapon from a bag . . .). The entire sequence suggests, of course, the idea of hypocrisy. But there is another idea that effectively comes through, and that has to do with the consecration of Michael's power. While his son is being baptized to life, Mike is being baptized to power. The role of godfather which he will play from this point on is a projection of his role as a parent. The power to give death is of a piece with the power to give life. Using them both, Michael grants his family survival. With uncanny though unself-conscious precision, *The Godfather* has captured the essence of the Mafia myth. It has bought into it and sold it to the world. But it has also changed it. Let's focus on this change.

The first consideration to be made is that the social identity of Mafia is originally characterized by a "regional" quality. With the migration to America, this quality becomes obsolete and the over- all identity needs to adapt accordingly. The enemy is no longer the foreign invader or the continental relative, but the local sys- tem within which the Mafia itself is recast as the foreign element. Separated from its roots, it now has to measure up against a stan- dard of success set by others. Aggression against and assimilation within the system proceed together in redefining the culture of the organization. *The Godfather* portrays this new scenario and develops it toward a dramatically cogent outcome. The film sets out to be no less than the "completion" of the myth.

Michael Corleone, a man who had not chosen crime but was pulled into it to save the family's honor, struggles his whole life to achieve one goal: to become legitimate. He wants to take his immigrant family to the other side of the road. Ironically, he will find that the world of finance and politics is not less treacherous or evil, and that the loss of innocence can be hidden but not reversed. In this sense, the film is an exploration of the "Balzac principle" according to which behind every great fortune lies a great crime (which Mario Puzo uses as an epigraph in the novel). The film explores how this original sin will always come back to haunt the perpetrator or his spawn. Coping with this destiny is the Godfather's tragedy. Although legitimacy turns out to be impossible, there is no safe return to the homeland for Michael either. Too much has happened to him and the society he oper- ates within. The future is a scam, the past fades away. The inescapable outcome is a moral disintegration: the unity of the family, the integration of crime and legitimate business, the forced cohabitation of opposite principles – violence and love – in Michael's ethos. It all eventually explodes in an operatic crescendo. Crossing the ocean, the myth has reached its natural culminating point. It has become bigger and more tragic, taking on the larger implications of cultural displacement.

Business: Michael (Al Pacino), McCluskey (Sterling Hayden), Sollozzo (Al Lettieri). *The Godfather* (1972), Copyright Paramount Pictures, 1972. Courtesy of the Museum of Modern Art Film Stills Archive

The definition of sexual roles is a crucial area through which *The Godfather* rewrites the book on the Mafia. Ostensibly, the mafioso is a monogamous, virtuous man who keeps his wife out of his business but provides for her every need. She in turn doesn't need much and is happy to stay in the backstage. Passion burns fiercely in the private, but needs no advertisement: the mafioso's ideal demeanor is a sort of "understated machismo." Hollywood filters this myth not only through a level of objectivity, but through the built-in rules of the crime genre. In the tradition of gangster films, the criminal heroes (or antiheroes) relate to women in a variety of pathological ways. There is a possessive pathology, by which women are trophies to be bought, safely kept, displayed in the proper situations, and discarded when they "go out of style." There is pathological jealousy, by which every perceived threat to this "property" becomes a direct threat to credibility, honor, and power of the man. There is a pathological transfer of incestuous desire (for the mother or the sister) to the other women, who are ultimately despised for not living up to "the real thing." There is a massive displacement of sexual tension into violence, a tendency that compounds the actual psychology of the criminal subject with the needs of the film industry vis-à-vis censorship. One of the great achievements of *The Godfather* is that it criticizes the Mafia myth without succumbing to these patterns of the genre.

In Coppola's trilogy, in fact, we have a broad range of relationships between the sexes. There is the devotion of Vito, the original Don, to his equally devoted, low-key Italian wife. There is the cold-hearted deception perpetrated by Michael at the expense of Kay, his well-educated American wife. There is the infidelity of Sonny, symptomatic of the lack of self-control that will be his undoing. There is the ambiguous seduction of Mary by Vincent, who ultimately gives her up to obtain his power. And there is a supporting cast of physically abusive husbands, embittered widows, and so forth. The overall picture is rich and complex. But we can easily spot a trend of deterioration that goes through the trilogy, both in the whole environment and in the central character's own conjugal affairs.

Michael starts off being open and communicative with Kay, concerned with shielding her from the ugly side of his family's activities but not cynical or duplicitous. As he comes to assume a position of leadership, his attitude changes to an extreme degree. He becomes hard, impenetrable, capable of lying without flinching about his own brother's murder. Kay is progressively imprisoned within the boundaries of the family's residences, and within the lie that she is forced to "believe." The problem is, she hasn't grown up in the acceptance of the Mafia value system; in fact, she isn't even Sicilian. She represents a corrupting agent within the organism of the family, and Michael has no choice but to build a wall of lies around her. Her way of breaking out of this existential quagmire is to abort the Godfather's child (a son). This gesture epitomizes Michael's failure to keep violence and disharmony out of his personal life. In the effort to protect his own family ties from the outside, he lets them weaken inside. This parable is universally understandable, and directly opposite to the essence of the original Mafia myth. Coppola wins on both counts: he makes the characters accessible *and* he takes them out of the stereotype. The relationship of Michael and Kay is not built around the specific sexual pathologies that typify the criminal mind, but around issues that we all can relate to. The marriage started with a 1950s-like definition of the roles. The dream of domestic bliss and prosperity is shattered by the awareness of the price to pay, a sentiment of disillusionment that seems integral to the sixties. Kay's behavior evokes a proto-feminist rejection of traditional roles (which is particularly impossible to accept from the standpoint of an Italian-American "man of honor"). It all ends in an escalation of emotional violence that is appropriately suited for the age of divorce. Once the family has broken, the third film proceeds inexorably toward the final disaster.

Coppola has brilliantly modulated the shifting mood of the saga through the use of light and color. In the first film, in which relationships are carried on under the aegis of filial love, loyalty, the cohesive power of patriarchal order (so much so that some critics have read into it a consistency of values with the so-called Silent Majority), the chiaroscuro is softer. Symbolically, darkness is not the space of unspeakable horror but the warm, womblike envelope that protects the silent ceremonies of men. Clarens observed how through the Venetian blinds filters an amber light, with the classic glow of an old painting. But in the second film, Michael is progressively swallowed up in darkness. His face is often half-lit, his presence tends to recede in the darker parts of the frame as he becomes more and more a dramatic enigma, and the film ends with a door shutting between him and Kay. In the third, the color scheme veers into operatic heights. The life of the Godfather has become opulent, but it ends in a personal catastrophe anticipated by the mise-en-scène of an actual opera (*La Cavalleria Rusticana*).

Michael Corleone ends up a lonely man; but this conclusion

doesn't just correspond to the classic trope of the king's solitude among men who are not his peers. It speaks to us of the dissolution of the dreams of youth, and the dreams of the sixties. Although the tradition of the gangster film required a hero that we as an audience could clearly constitute as "other" from us – pathological, morally reproachable – so as to reinforce our identity by opposition, *The Godfather* gives us a man that we want to be, or that we can't help being. As much as we enjoyed his affirmations of power (carefully set up in the film as righteous revenges, almost supernatural in their efficiency), we empathize with his suffering the consequences.

In the last analysis, *The Godfather* has made the Mafia myth speak to us of us. It has made the myth mainstream, and so it has made it permeable to the influences of popular culture. This leads us to the next question: how has the Mafia itself absorbed the change?

By becoming an international organization worthy of such media attention, and of such glorification as *The Godfather* bestowed on it, the Mafia has at least partially abdicated its "telluric" prerogative. It has outgrown its ties to the land, and the relative value system. Once it became immersed in the international drug trade, once its ethnic identity became diluted, and most importantly, once it engaged in self-representation on this level, the Mafia entered into a new, very different stage of its history. Ultimately, its very identity is at stake. The psychology of the peasant who resorts to crime in front of an absentee or corrupt government isn't the same as the immigrant trying to make his mark by any means necessary, and it certainly isn't the same as the third-generation descendant who sees his life glamorized by movie stars. For the past twenty-five years, the mafioso has had the opportunity to look at movies that made his life big, powerful, glamorous, and complex enough to provide the audience not just a vicarious thrill, but an inspiration: he couldn't help wanting that life. And so the real mafiosi began taking after their on-screen counterparts at the same time they were inspiring them. Even if most movies depicted them as cruel and unrefined, the classy aura of *The Godfather* seemed to stick to the role enough to make this semiotic exchange possible. Eventually, the language of the movies, the language of the news, and the language of the Mafia combined in the creation of a new gestalt: Dons became "dapper," high-rolling, large-living, media-conscious, and vain. They became celebrities.

John Gotti, the most prominent American mafioso of recent years, is the exemplary product of this evolution – as flamboyant and overtly aggressive as his Sicilian predecessors were (or pretended to be) subtle and conniving. The difference between Carlo Gambino, the uncredited model for *The Godfather* – who was small, stooped, and completely inconspicuous in his clothes and demeanor – and John Gotti, notorious for his $2,000 custom-made De Lisi suits and his very short temper, couldn't be more striking. Armand Assante, who played Gotti in the HBO movie, was the right actor for the job: extroverted, narcissistic, prone to let his undeniable talent roam loose. In the film, the older mafiosi reproach him time and again for courting the headlines. But Gotti knows that his charisma is built on flash, bravado, TV-friendly looks; he knows he's riding the wave of fashion. He probably knows (the film hints at this, but doesn't quite grasp the full tragic potential of the idea) that his popularity will eventually exact the highest price. To his credit, he'll be willing to pay it – a stand-up attitude that the film celebrates in its bookends.

As a result of the change in perception we have discussed, strategic retreats into a low profile became virtually impossible: after taking center stage in such a successful way, how could the Mafia cultivate again the Machiavellian skill of operating behind the scenes?

In general, these past twenty-five years of Mafia history show us how the organization became addicted to consumerism, became shallow and nihilistic – how it lost faith in the once cogent fiction of its "code": honor, respect, silence. Whereas in the previous era it would have been extraordinary for a mafioso to betray the organization, it is now common. In addition to the immediate damage, the consequences are devastating to the myth itself. Given its mimetic faculties and its innate ability to occupy the interstices of political power, the Mafia has proven hard to kill, and it has developed a mystique of invulnerability. However, what we see clearly now is that the Mafia can and will defeat itself; the organism can be harmed most severely from the inside. Not only does every defection provoke a chain reaction of divisive revenges and ulterior defections, but it destroys the cultural fabric, the very "soul" of the Mafia.

By acquiring and enjoying visibility, the Mafia has lost the principal source of its power, that is, secrecy. This loss is catastrophic. First, because secrecy used to allow the mafiosi to live in the open, and commit crimes on the sly – without rescinding their social ties, but simply lying about them. Exposure forced them to become fully clandestine – a form of secrecy that is purely tactical as opposed to ontological, imposed by the enemy as opposed to chosen, a function of shame and fear as opposed to proud exclusivity. Second, because there is a cohesive strength that is tempered in secrecy; there are a symbolic resonance and an intellectual cachet that come with it. The more an organization operates in the shadow, the more it can stretch its symbolic roots deep into the past, and project itself into the future. But exposure is definition, and therefore *limitation*. The mindset that made a good mafioso was the unwillingness to ask direct questions, and the ability to say without saying. Not only did that make investigators impotent, but it gave the mafioso a semantic arsenal like no other. Any word could be charged with the highest power, mean everything and its opposite, be a pure manifestation of will – and so could any silence. (The original lingo of the mafioso is called *baccagghiu*, which means "speaking in riddles.") The move to America has forced the mafiosi, or those who would become such, to learn a new language, dilute their symbolic integrity, produce a new criminal esperanto that was open to the influence of other organizations, cultural trends, and the media at large. The media have said too much, solved all the riddles, and made Mafia's semantic control irretrievable. Now the mafioso is typecast, marketed, consumed – he's made to speak in a language he doesn't quite own, and which he is rather *owned by*.

It is significant in this respect that Mario Puzo chose to bring the Mafia into Hollywood in his novel *The Last Don*. Although the novel is old-fashioned and far removed from the true goings-on of recent Mafia history, in a mythical sense the kingdom of glitz is the appropriate stage for the shenanigans of modern mafiosi. Hollywood is, after all, a place where moral aberrations are nothing but potential scandals, and the measure of power is not in setting the standards but in controlling the spin – power itself being admittedly impermanent. Even in Italy, the battlefield where the Mafia now fights – and where it's being defeated – is so public, and so deliberately used for spectacle, that the spiral of crime-punishment-retaliation seems to be entirely determined by the needs of the media. After the introduction of legislation that prescribes maximum security and minimum privilege prison time for members of La Cosa Nostra, the organization was so eager for a reaction carrying the highest possible shock value that it started attacking the national artistic treasures (most notably, bombing the Uffizi Gallery in Florence). The message seemed to be: if the unwritten rules of this war are modified by the state, if chaos is unleashed, then we'll multiply the chaos. Everybody will suffer, except the media. But the most exhibitionistic stunt in the war was scored by the government. During the airing of a TV movie about the Mafia murder of Judge Giovanni Falcone in May 1996, on the state-sponsored national network Rai 1, an announcement appeared at the bottom of the screen announcing that Giovanni Brusca had just been captured. Brusca was the last man involved in the Falcone murder still on the lam. He was watching the movie in his secret hideout. The police had known about it for days and timed the capture for best TV exposure. When the news broke, policemen drove around noisily in a self-congratulatory celebration. Brusca, who was indicted for over one hundred homicides including the teenage son of an informer, whose body he dissolved in acid, turned informer himself.

The whole scenario is a remarkable example of how media feedback interacts with a social phenomenon and alters its course. The Mafia has spawned a genre of the popular arts, and the genre has redefined the Mafia to the point of threatening its existence – or the conditions of its existence. The final question is, then, What does it mean in a broader sociological sense that crime has become such a "cultural commodity" as to be reinvented by the media?

Rather than attempting an answer here, I would content myself to phrase and posit the question in a thought-provoking way. The vast debate on violence in the media has rarely plunged below the surface of the issue. While the prophets of our imminent return to savagery, the V-chip advocates, and the NC-17 supporters are horrified at how the media flirt with crime and end up inspiring it, we should adopt a much broader standpoint. Crime is today inseparable from its representation. Terrorism is but a form of advertisement; organized crime is a form of politics, of public administration; individual crime is an attempt at renegotiating one's image among other images. Crime has developed an aesthetic dimension. It can be "chilling," "horrific," "elaborate," and "ritualistic," like the murders of a serial killer. (The definition itself is a product of the media; technically, serial killers have always been there, but every murder is just another murder without public recognition of a linkage. At the same time, media recognition is one of the serial killer's motivating rewards.) Also, crime can be "barbaric," "outrageous," "atrocious," "apocalyptic" like a wartime massacre (and references would be made to Dante's Inferno, the paintings of Bosch, etc.). It can be "mindless," "random," "numbing," like a "gang-related drive-by shooting." (This very expression seems to automatically evoke a whole scene complete with its own soundtrack.) In fact, we expect crime to have a look, a feel, a sound – both on its own and through the appropriate media coverage. We cannot conceive it outside this *gestalt:* it is a spectacle that we were born with. Even the hardest anticrime, antiviolence in the media speakers exploit the evocative power that crime has derived from the media.

Cinema is one of the agents that give shape to this aesthetic dimension, and the artistic choices that such a role entails are now more conscious and sophisticated than ever. As there are no rigid genres to conform to, each film is free to create its own moral world, its own philosophy of crime. Tarantino's *Pulp Fiction* is a fascinating example: a film in which bad guys are redeemed by the interaction with worse guys, and violence can be "cool," funny, or ugly as the story needs.

The Godfather marked a seminal moment in our cultural history because it embraced the responsibility of these choices and didn't simplify them to the point where Mafia would have to be either "condemned" or "glorified," Its ultimate achievement is exactly this "double movement," ambiguous as the Mafia itself, of critique and reaffirmation of the Mafia myth.

3 The Representation of Ethnicity in *The Godfather*

To an Italian-American, "compare" means "godfather." . . . Traditionally, a godfather means an alter ego in place of a parent in time of need. The picture *The Godfather* has had the effect of changing the meaning. Henceforth, the term Godfather will be understood to mean a ruthless Italian killer.

(Patrick Gallo, *Old Bread, New Wine*)

The way some people link every Italian to the Mafia in a half joking way does not bother me. Actually, the Mafia has always been considered glamorous. I don't know why people find bullies that glamorous, yet it seems to be an unending source of fascination to Americans. . . . Some things have reached a level of the classic.

(Frank Stella, artist, *Growing Up Italian*)

In writing about their cultural experience, members of the Italian-American community often regret the way they are stereotypically linked with organized crime in the American imagination.[1] And it is Francis Ford Coppola's immensely popular *Godfather* trilogy that is perceived as being most influential in securing this criminal image.[2] Although some Italian Americans are deeply offended by the association, others, like Frank Stella, for example, seem to take a distance from it. Stella observes that the brutal image of the Mafia is also a marketable and glamorous one. Critically speaking, however, the insight that the representation of crime is attractive is not new, nor is the fact that it has made for centuries of popular entertainment.[3] But what is of interest is to consider why the specifically *Italian-American* criminal has been so fascinating, and why *The Godfather* is such a significant example of that fascination.

To this end, this chapter discusses *The Godfather,* and does so in terms of its Italianicity[4] – that is, in terms of the accepted cultural codes that are inscribed in the three films of this series to render the notion of "Italianness." It is not my intention, however, to consider this quality in terms of its "correctness" – that is, as to whether or not it constitutes an accurate or true representation of Italian Americans. Instead, this chapter discusses how these codes have been utilized to create a *particular type* of Italian American, one fashioned for a specific time in American history. *The Godfather* films, especially *Parts I* and *II,* readily lend themselves to this analysis since the codes for Italianicity occupy their "epidermal" surface,[5] and take as a central theme the order and power of traditional Italian ways in confrontation with the corroding effects of America. But this surface ethnicity (it must be noted that ethnicity, as it is used here, is not a fixed entity, but a shifting construct responding to historical, sociological, and cultural changes)[6] is only an apparent one. The chapter also investigates the "submerged ethnicity" in the films – that is, the ethnicity that is not always clearly stated, yet which results in an interplay of ethnic voices,[7] ones instrumental in the creation of the Italian American as criminal image. It is to these voices, then, whose wishes and needs the film also speaks, that this chapter directs its attention. In this way, it will become apparent that the Italian-American criminal in *The Godfather* is a construct fashioned to the needs and the dictates of a society at a distinct period in American history.

THE GODFATHER PARTS I AND II

In an essay titled "Reification and Utopia in Mass Culture," Fredric Jameson writes:

. . . all contemporary works of art – whether those of high culture and modernism or of mass culture – have as their underlying impulse – albeit in what is often distorted and repressed unconscious form – our deepest fantasies about the nature of social life, both as we live it now, and as we feel in our bones it ought rather be lived.[8]

Since *The Godfather* centers around the image of family life – one lived, above all, in cooperation, love, and commitment – it has often been noted that this film forms for us a collective wish for something that has been lost in American life.[9] This is the surface wish, however, the most apparent socially fulfilling value that these film have, especially at the time of their original release in 1972 and 1974, an era that saw not only the disintegration of the family, but also the deterioration of America's faith in government. After the societal unrest of the 1960s and the war in Vietnam, *The Godfather* presents an illusion of family unity, as well as the purposeful and justified use of violence by an organized group. Just at a time when the American government was perceived as being the perpetrator of unjust acts, the films can be seen as accomplishing a satisfying collective fantasy of legitimized violence.[10]

The question that I would now like to ask of this often noted interpretation is: *How* was such a fantasy constructed from the image of Italian-American characters and from an elaborate cinematic construction meant to connote "Italianicity"? And, in addition, *why*, of all the possible ethnicities within American society, was the Italian American able to create this satisfying effect within a popular form of entertainment?

Authenticity

First, it must be noted that *The Godfather* brings to us, like perhaps no other film before it in American film history, the notion of "authenticity"[11] when presenting Italian Americans as an ethnic group. Not only are its director, Francis Ford Coppola, and its writer, Mario Puzo, Italian Americans, but so are many of the actors and actresses cast in the film's ethnic roles. In addition,

The young Italian immigrant, Vito Corleone (Robert DeNiro), and his family. *The Godfather Part II* (1974), Copyright Paramount Pictures, 1974. Courtesy of the Museum of Modern Art Film Stills Archive

the film is constructed with an elaborate attention to detail, presenting a rich layering of images, sounds, and gestures meant to connote an authentic ethnic type. The ultimate effect of this construction is one of a true Italian-American voice, an insider's view, as it were, spoken by people who know "the grit," as was claimed by Paramount executive Robert Evans when promoting the film.[12] What must be acknowledged, however, is that this very notion of "authenticity" is part of the film's construction, part of its symbolic surface, its weave of illusion.

To dismantle this notion of authenticity, then, let us begin by addressing the issue of a true Italian-American voice. To this end it should be noted that neither Coppola nor Puzo is an authentic voice for the life of the Sicilian Mafia family represented in the film. Puzo is a writer of northern Italian heritage rather than a Sicilian (the distinction between northern and southern Italy is one that provides a profound cultural distinction within Italian society) and so had little first-hand knowledge of the culture he embodied in his book. According to Puzo's own claim,[13] he extensively researched the culture of southern Italy and the Mafia for *The Godfather*, but he was not part of it himself. In addition, before the book was published by G. P. Putnam & Sons, Paramount Pictures producer Al Ruddy bought the film rights to the novel, helped to shape it, and eventually slated it for production. In terms of ethnicity, then, Paramount and its executives must be seen as additional influences, or voices, speaking through the film,[14] and ones that serve to dilute the claim of an unmediated Italian-American authenticity.

It was also Paramount executives, men such as Ruddy and Evans, who soon considered various directors for *The Godfather*. And although Coppola was eventually offered the project, his southern Italian heritage seems not to have been a primary consideration in the search. In fact, the film had first been offered to Arthur Penn and Costa Gavras,[15] among others, all non-Italian-American directors who subsequently turned down the project. Coppola too was far from seeing the proposed film as a vehicle for his true "Italian self" and had initially recoiled from the project. He told his father, Carmine Coppola, the composer who once worked with Arturo Toscanini, that he thought the script was "trash." The young Coppola had wanted to make his own films, to make art, but now his independent film studio, American Zoetrope, was near bankruptcy and he needed the money. So, it was to save his studio that Francis Coppola finally consented to direct *The Godfather* as a work-for-hire.

Although Coppola may have first perceived *The Godfather* as "trash," what he was actually being asked to direct was a gangster film, a lowly genre that had been stagnant for years. And one of the *conventions* of this genre, almost from its inception, has been its claim for authenticity, for its connection to the "real." This convention came into vogue when Warner Brothers, the studio that produced the early gangster films *Little Caesar* (1930) and *Scarface* (1932), took as its motto and proudly proclaimed the "Snatched from Today's Headlines" authenticity[16] of its pictures.

And to this end, both of these films represented Italian-American criminals, with *Scarface,* in particular, being a thinly disguised rendition of the real-life Al Capone. But, of course, not all crime was Italian, and so James Cagney played Tom Powers, an Irish-American gangster in the popular film *Public Enemy* (1933). Regardless of the claims for authenticity, however, it was the Hays Code that finally ended the tendency to cinematically link a particular ethnic group to crime. In 1933 the Production Code limited the type of content permitted in Hollywood film. In Section 10 of the Code, under the heading "National Feeling," the injunction stated: ". . . no picture shall be produced that tends to indicate bigotry or hatred among people of differing races, religions, or national origins."

The films that followed this injunction in the 1930s and 1940s largely removed the specific connection between organized crime and ethnicity. But the Hays Code was to change the gangster film in even more profound ways. Since the Code had restricted the representation of crime and violence as well, the genre needed to be altered to emphasize the triumph of the law over the forces of evil. To this end, the criminal was no longer allowed to occupy the central position in the films. Instead, that position was reserved for the lawman, or later, for the detective, a change that expanded the genre into the Thriller and the Film Noir categories. Although an Italian name would occasionally appear in these films, such as "Canino" in *The Big Sleep* (1946) or "Johnny Rocco" in *Key Largo,* the elaborate connection to an ethnic community was not made.

The Hays Code, however, was not able to indefinitely maintain its control over the content of the Hollywood film. With the demise of the studio system in the 1950s, the Hays Code progressively lost its power over the content of film production. So eventually, with films like *Al Capone* (1959), *The St. Valentine's Day Massacre* (1967), and Paramount's *The Brotherhood* (1969), the gangster returned, as did his explicit and elaborated ethnicity. But even with all the attempted explicitness, there is little in these films that feels like an "authentic" ethnic representation. When compared to *The Godfather*, the ethnic inflections – the gestures, the accents, the decor, the dialogue, the costumes – in short, "the grit" – here seem somehow paper thin and unconvincing. In a very apparent way, the voices that are heard in these films are much more "white" than they are Italian.

The Godfather, then, must be seen as an important moment in the evolution of the gangster genre. This film accomplishes an elaborate *return*, now not only to the gangster genre, but to the old-style gangster film, one complete with the criminal as a central character, and with the convention of the Italian-American criminal. Unlike any earlier attempts at this return, however, *The Godfather* expands the gangster story and the representation of ethnicity beyond all previous renditions. A new type of Italian-American gangster is presented here, one that is well researched and is set in works that are superbly directed, acted, art directed, shot, and scored. But, nonetheless, this gangster is one constructed for a specific period in American history. It must also be noted that the films' particular mix of new insights and old conventions is a combination that proved almost irresistible to the viewing public. In fact, *The Godfather* was the highest grossing motion picture of its time, with *Parts I and II* subsequently combined and viewed as a TV miniseries by 132 million people. What's more, the films not only proved popular with the general public, but were also reputedly esteemed by members the Mafia itself.[17]

Italianicity

What kind of Italian American does *The Godfather* bring to us? Perhaps the best way to understand the importance of *The Godfather*'s particular brand of Italianicity is to compare it to similar codes of ethnicity in the original Howard Hawks's film, *Scarface*. This is an especially apt comparison since *Scarface* is also the film that best embodies the old genre conventions that *The Godfather* simultaneously returns to and then expands on. By comparing these two films, we will be better able to appreciate the important position that *The Godfather* holds in the evolution of the

Mafia consensus: The families make up. Vito Corleone (Brando) and Barzini (Richard Conte), applauding. *The Godfather* (1972). Copyright Paramount Pictures, 1972. Courtesy of the Museum of Modern Art Film Stills Archive

gangster film, and to acknowledge the importance of their distinct historical period. This will be especially crucial when comparing the ethnic representations in the two films. Here the temptation is to assess one of the films' screen Italians as being more true or real than the other. The emphasis, however, should be on the period in American history when these films were made. In this way, both *Scarface* and *The Godfather* will be seen as true and complete discourses,[18] but ones responding to a different set of historical and cultural conditions.

Scarface, made in 1932, betrays a very different attitude toward the Italian ethnic than does *The Godfather*. In the original *Scarface*, Tony Camonte is presented as a brutal criminal, but his looks and demeanor also evoke the image of a petulant child. The ugly scar on Camonte's cheek refers to the violence of the real-life Al Capone, while the full lips, fleshy face, and brashly determined actions bring out the child, as well as the "demon in the child." Tony is a primitive who wants what he wants, and he'll literally stop at nothing to get it. What's more, this Tony is of Italian origin, as his mother, dressed in peasant costume, is there to attest to. Rendered as a recent immigrant, Tony's mother speaks with a near-Vaudeville Italian accent,[19] a mode of speech shared by Tony himself. Mama Camonte is also meant to evoke a particular Italian physical type. Here she is presented as a drab woman, with dark frazzled hair surrounding her almost mannish face. The markers for Italianicity in *Scarface*, then, are primarily in tags of character, such as in the presentation of Italian names, the rendition of costume, the accents of the characters' speech, as well as in the attention to the physical characteristics of a proposed ethnic "type." These elements, however, are constructed with a kind of derision that complies more closely with the position of the Italian ethnic in American society in the late 1920s and early 1930s. Removed only a few decades from the category of recent immigrants and hated minority, these representations bespeak a cultural bias created by the "white" film makers, and dominant society as well. In this film, Italianicity is an added marker for Camonte's primitive depravity. Tony is childish, not educated (although deviously intelligent), a kind of buffoon, but also brutal in a way that bespeaks not a hint of remorse or morality. That he is also Italian completes the picture, or better still, explains it. Tony Camonte is a lower human type, and one characterized by explosive and violent passions.

But it must be added that this image, rather than being all bad, is one that audiences found profoundly attractive at the film's release, and one that has made *Scarface* a classic of film history. Camonte is attractive and popular for the same reasons that the real-life Al Capone had reached cult-hero status during this historical period.[20] For the Depression era, the fantasy of the self-made man, the man who would stop at nothing to get what he wanted, was perceived as satisfying. And the fact that Camonte was of Italian origin actually worked to sustain this illusion. Although it may have reduced him in moral stature, it also made him accessible, and so constructed an (albeit tainted) everyman for consumption by the viewing audience.

But Tony Camonte's is not the only Italian-American voice ostensibly presented in *Scarface*. In a later section of the film, one that was added to please the censors, a "real" Italian immigrant is allowed to speak. Rather than the flamboyant vulgarity of Camonte, this man is recondite, darkly attired, and older. His deeply furrowed face quivers as he speaks English with a now more modified Italian accent. Decrying the glorification of violence and criminality in the media, he worries about the bad effect that this image may have on Italian Americans. He says of these criminal representations: ". . . They bring nothing but shame to my people."

The implication here, of course, and one planted by the film makers to squelch objections from concerned members of the community, is that not all Italian Americans are criminals, that most Italians are good people. But this preachy segment fails to achieve its intended effect. As far as the film as a whole is concerned, Tony Camonte is a much more appealing character than this failed, timorous little Italian man. It is, after all, Tony Camonte whom we have paid to see.

Although *The Godfather Parts I and II* are separated from *Scarface* by some forty years, they continue many of the traditions noted in the earlier film. Here again we have a brutal Italian-American gangster with almost universal appeal, and one who occupies a central position in the films. Whether played by Marlon Brando, Al Pacino, or Robert DiNiro, the films' characters, Vito and Michael Corleone, are among the best loved and most well known in the history of American film. But even though these similarities can be noted, the question still remains: What are the differences between the earlier representations of Italian-American gangsters and the one presented in *The Godfather?*

First, it must be acknowledged that the codes for Italianicity in *The Godfather* films are not only presented as embellishments of character as they were in *Scarface,* but that they also represent one of the films' major themes. This is evident from the very first scene of *The Godfather*. The film starts with the verbal account by an Italian-American everyman, an honorably man dressed somberly in black, whose story encapsulates many of the primary tensions of the film. As the man begins to speak in the typical, but now refined, speech of an Italian immigrant, a close-up camera steadily recedes to encompass the surrounding dark space. "I believe in America" are his first words. He continues in counterpoint, describing how the deterioration of traditional Italian ways by all things American has ended by destroying his only daughter, his hope in the future. This man's daughter dated an American, stayed out late, as is the American way, and was eventually brutalized by this boy, who disfigured her, and by the American legal system that knows neither true honor nor justice. For this reason, the man has come to the Godfather to ask for help and to find justice in the rules of the old Sicilian ways. A reverse shot finally reveals Vito Corleone seated before this humble man, listening to his story with composure and assumed power.

In an article titled "*Godfather II:* A Deal Coppola Couldn't Refuse," John Hess[21] argues that *The Godfather*, by extending this theme of the corrosive influence of American society across especially *Part II* of the film, eventually accomplishes a critique of capitalism itself. This critique is accomplished, Hess contends, by the film's contrapuntal structure which dramatizes the progressive deterioration of the family by the ravaging effects of American's dominant ideology. The film's opening sequence presents a premonition of this deterioration of the family under America's destructive effects, but one that is salvaged by the still intact power of the Don. By the end of *Part II*, however, the Corleone family too finds its demise. This is demonstrated by Michael's stupendous business and criminal success, and by the simultaneous destruction of his cherished Italian family. Although Hess's is a very insightful piece, I would here like to supply an additional reading for the film, one made accessible both by analyzing the surface representation of ethnicity in *The Godfather* and by looking at its "submerged" ethnicity as well – that is, to the non-Italian and very American voices. Here a countercurrent to Hess's reading will become apparent, one that not so much critiques capitalism, but rather exalts it.

To this end, another important scene needs to be discussed in *Part II* of *The Godfather*. Set in the 1910 Vito Corleone section of the film, Vito and a friend go to the theater to see a play about the New York life of an Italian immigrant. (It is interesting to note that this play, "Senza Mamma," was originally written by Francis Coppola's maternal grandfather, Francesco Pennino,[22] at the early part of the twentieth century, and so presents a true Italian immigrant voice within the film.) Highly melodramatic, the play portrays a man in his tenement kitchen, with the Statue of Liberty visible outside the painted backdrop window. The man receives a letter informing him of his mother's death in Italy. As Vito watches the stage from his theater seat, we, the audience, watch the film in ours, and from this vantage point we can make a comparison between the man on stage and Vito himself. For the stage character, his mother's death means the loss of Italy, the old life, the old warmth. For the immigrant, this past has been tragically replaced by a two-dimensional Statue of Liberty, and a hope that has resulted only in an impoverished tenement and the disconnection from one's roots. In his rage and despair, this good and honorable man turns to violence. But here he vents this violence against himself, raising a pistol to his head at the play's end. It must be noted, however, that this sequence condenses almost all of the motivating forces within the life of the young Vito Corleone himself. Vito too had looked with mixed emotion at the Statue of Liberty outside his Ellis Island window; he too had found a meager existence and was forced to live in a tenement flat, and he too had lost his mother. Unlike the stage character, however, Vito does not respond with a desperate act of self-destruction.

Vito's mother had been brutally murdered before his eyes, and the violent propulsion of her body in response to the gunshot blast was the force that catapulted him into the new world. Now because of the injustice done to him and his loved ones, Vito vents his anger outward. He shoots the villain, Fanucci, the same type of villain who had murdered his mother, and who now threatens a young girl, as well as Vito and his family. Fanucci dies in a brutally excessive, but exhilarating, act of *displaced vengeance.* With the years of controlled rage finally released, Vito's action is experienced as a justifiable and liberating use of violence.

So again in *The Godfather* we see this notion of a "return." Not only does the film return us to an old genre, with old-style Italian gangsters, but on many levels of its construction it utilizes the notion of returning to *older* or outmoded forms and practices. It is important to note here that this particular use of violence, one perpetrated by a vigilante to protect the weak against the tyrannical, returns us not only to primitive stages of civilized society, but also to one of the original practices of the Mafia itself. In fact, it is in this type of activity that the Sicilian Mafia was first born.[23] Long before the Mafia's descent into crime, the early bands of mafiosi were protectors of the people against villains, the only recourse in a land ravaged by foreign invaders and feudal landlords. Without a strong government of their own, or a strong legal system, these mafiosi became the "enemies of enemies," and wielded a kind of primitive, or "frontier," law for the peasants. *The Godfather's* first manipulation, then (as exemplified by Vito's original act of violence in *Part II*), is to diminish the character's association with the realities of a crime organization and to *return* them to a practice closer to the origins of the Mafia: to a rendition of the Mafia as alternate law giver.

The Godfather's Italians are different from other film representations of this ethnic group because they also embody a return to "La Via Vecchia,"[24] or to the old Sicilian ways. The Italian Americans who are constructed here are ones who embody the mores of an ancient society, and so take on a nostalgic quality. It must be stressed that *La Via Vecchia* is a Sicilian term used to describe ways of behaving, of thinking, and of organizing one's life, and one that has a bearing on the rules of comportment for men, women, and the members of the family. It is through the clash of these ways with the encroachments of American society, then, that this film enacts its major codes of Italianicity.

The representation of the Italian-American male in *The God-*

father is different from earlier renditions in that it incorporates an older, almost chivalrous mode of behavior into its image. In so doing, it contests the standing stereotypes for the Italian-American male. Although varying across the century, this stereotype has ranged from the man of excessive passion for sex or violence, to the dumb fool, stumbling over his words and often getting a laugh.[25] Tony Carmonte's excesses in choice of clothes and jewelry, for example, as well as his greedy violence and silly speech, certainly comply with this pattern. The rules of comportment for the southern Italian male,[26] however, describe a very different type of individual, and one that is much closer to the way that Vito and Michael Corleone in *The Godfather Parts I and II* are constructed. The description of the ideal southern Italian male is a creature of control, *"un uomo di pazienza"* (a man of patience), a man who holds his body erect, but composed, his face impassive, and who plans, waits, and then acts. He is not a man of brash impulse, or of too many, or of ill-chosen, words. Nor is he a man of public romantic or sexual display. What's more, this Sicilian level of control, this machismo, is far from being an indicator of vacuity, or of a shallowness of feeling. It is, in fact, its opposite. The depth of passion is here controlled and then directed, and so results in power.

In *The Godfather*, Vito and Michael Corleone behave in this manner, one that bespeaks and supports their worldly power. Sonny Corleone, however, does not. And it is precisely this breach of the Sicilian code of manliness that weakens him and leaves him vulnerable to attack. In fact, it is "La Via Vecchia" that occupies a symbolic central position within the film, dictating the behavior of all of its men, and thus defining the limits of masculinity and the limits of culpability as well. The villainous male characters in the film are guilty and punishable to the degree that they deviate from these established codes of honor. In this way, *The Godfather* diminishes the characters' association with crime and its squalid realities, and instead foregrounds acts made punishable precisely because they are reactions against the breach of an ancient masculine code. A good man's code of honor, for example, extends to his commitment to his family and to his respect of women and of the law. Within the logic of the film, then, those who commit an "infamia" deserve all they get. So, since Woltz is a foul-mouthed despoiler of young girls, and McClusky is a vulgar cop who violates the law, and Carlo is a wife beater and a traitor to his family, they become worthy of their punishment.

Power and righteousness come through control, and it is the man who is in complete control of himself and his actions who can then control his family and his business. It must be noted, however, that according to "La Via Vecchia," this man is not so much "in control" of his woman as he finds in her his counterpart. The man may be the head of his family, but the woman is its center.[27] As dictated by these old ways, the ideal woman is "La Donna di Serieta," a woman of seriousness, of dignity and virtue. Her domain is her household and her family, and everything revolves around her. Here again we are given a model for order maintained by an ancient society. This feminine ideal, then, is evidenced in *The Godfather* and forms the same poles of compliance and deviance that explain a character's worth within the film.

It has often been noted that the women represented in *The Godfather* are peripheral to the central actions of the film.[28] In many ways, however, this can be seen as a structuring absence, and one sustained by the dictates of "La Via Vecchia." Mama Corleone, for example, is certainly fashioned according to this ideal of womanliness. Portrayed by Morgana King with her regally graying hair, full figure, and matronly dresses, she is the embodiment of the mother as creator and maintainer of the family, and the center of all that Michael and Vito try so desperately to protect. Even as the young version of herself in *Part II*, Mama Corleone talks little (it is almost as if she withdraws from us, the prying eyes of the outside world), but she is the compelling reason for Vito's vengeful killing of Fanucci. It was, after all, Fanucci who had unjustly deprived Vito of his job and his ability to feed his family (in addition to threatening to slash the face of a beautiful young girl). In this way, the presence of many of the women in the film provide the ultimate justification for the represented acts of violence. It was the murder of Vito's mother, the threat to Kay as she slept in her own home, and even the disfiguring of the undertaker's daughter in the opening sequence, for example, that fueled and justified both the young and the old Don's actions.

But with the disintegration of the family, it is the behavior of the women that best signals its decline. After the murder of her husband, Connie loses her center, ignoring her children and indulging in multiple affairs and divorces. And after the death of Appolonia, the perfect wife of "La Via Vecchia," Michael marries Kay, a New England WASP who never really understands the codes for Sicilian womanliness. And it is this deviation from the norm that eventually results in Kay's demise, and her contribution to the destruction of her own family. Before her marriage, Kay had sexual relations with Michael, as well as being an independent working woman. And after their marriage, she continued this outsider behavior by repeatedly asking her husband about his business – to which she got the predictable answer. Mama Corleone had never asked Vito about his business because she knew better. Whether a southern Italian woman's husband is a baker, a fisherman, or a gangster, it would be considered unmanly for him to discuss his business with her.[29] Kay's divergence is, in fact, so profound that she is almost the inverse of the original Donna Andolini, Vito's mother. This fierce woman had once held a knife to Don Ciccio's throat with the full intention to commit murder in order save her son's life. Kay, instead, is *"una disgraziata"* who aborts her unborn son. Kay's behavior so profoundly destabilizes Michael that he loses control. He deteriorates his manhood by striking the woman who is also his wife and the mother of his children.

In *The Godfather* the codes of Italianicity carry the connotation for pastness on other levels as well. The music is the first promoter of this association, with the opening *Godfather* theme rich in sounds of the mandolin, an instrument and a melody that recall an earlier era as well as an older type of Italian – a turn-of-the-century Italian. The images and sounds of the old country, of Italy, serve to underline this pastness. Here Sicily is a rugged, barren land, heavy with broken rocks and ancient yet austere buildings. The diction and the gestures of the characters presented recall their earlier roots, either by speaking Italian in the dialect of southern Italy or, when in America, an English often marked by the accents of the recent immigrant, or by that of the working-class Italian American. The physical types of Italian Americans chosen for these roles also connote an earlier stage of cultural development. Clemenza as the sloe-eyed fat man, for example, or Pentangeli with his kindly manner and gravelly voice, or even Michael with his serene beauty, may seem "authentic," but it must be noted that they also belie an assumption of ethnic purity. In assembling a composite of Italian types, then, the Italian Americans in *The Godfather Parts I and II* connote a time before the more contemporary stages of ethnic assimilation.

Nostalgia

The tendency of *The Godfather*, then, is to return to past forms that are either in the process of fading away or have already done so. This tendency is apparent on many levels of the film. We have noted the film's return to the origins of the Mafia as an alternative form of law giver, and to the Old World codes of honor and comportment for both men and women. *The Godfather's* system of return also extends to the gangster genre itself and brings the genre back to a type of gangster that was more evident at the origins of the form in the 1930s, one who is featured as the central character of the film and who can claim an ethnic origin. But unlike those early movies that saw Italianness in terms of derision, *The Godfather's* Italian Americans are wistfully portrayed through the fading memory of "La Via Vecchia." Here, then, the primary meaning of the Italian American is no longer that of the lowly primitive. Instead, this ethnic type is rendered so that its very meaning is nostalgia – nostalgia for something lost, for something left behind. And it is in this tendency to return to the past that *The Godfather* fits into a category of postmodern film that Fredric Jameson has dubbed "Le Mode Retro," or the Nostalgia Film.

For Jameson, however, the nostalgia in postmodern films is present not only on the level of content, but on the level of image itself.[30] *The Godfather* complies here too with images of Italian-American settings and decor that are imbued with a quality of pastness. These images, however, not only represent scenes set in the past, but, as Jameson has noted, take on the very quality of images from that past era. To this end, Gordon Willis, the films' cinematographer, has described his intention to create a "Kodachromy, 1942 find of feel"[31] to the image, and so connote the pictures of an earlier period. This allusion to pastness is intensified in *The Godfather* by the dark interiors, the almost Rembrandt-inspired use of light, and the stillness of many of the figures represented within the shots. The allusion here (especially in the scenes of Vito Corleone's study where the men gather to discuss business) is to the stylistic qualities of Old Masters' paintings, and in the 1901 and 1917 New York sequences, to the faded quality of turn-of-the-century photographs portraying the lives of recent immigrants. Here, however, the former squalor and gritty realism evident in these pictures is seen through the golden light of warmth and nostalgia.

On the level of the image, then, *The Godfather* is very different from the early gangster film, *Scarface*. *Scarface*, of course, is the original, and only looks "old" in retrospect. *The Godfather*, on the other hand, actively *effects* a quality of pastness on the part of the image. But there is an important similarity between *The Godfather* and *Scarface* that must be noted, one that shows the newer film again alluding to its origins. As mentioned earlier, *Scarface* had difficulty getting by the censors, and the film's release was delayed until certain changes were made. The film was originally conceived to show Tony Camonte centrally featured and unmediated in his criminal activities. But this was considered too provocative, and so the moralists demanded that a written statement be included at the beginning of the film, one decrying the criminal and the representation of violence, and that additional supporting sequences be added. The effect of these proscribed changes was meant to disengage the viewers' identification with the criminal, and to instead position those viewers on the side of the law.[32]

From this vantage point, the audience is encouraged to interpret the criminal events as despicable and dangerous and as evils that must be stopped.

The Godfather differs from this censored approach and is closer to *Scarface* as it was originally conceived. Like the older film, *The Godfather* does not position the viewers on the side of the law, but rather securely engages them on the side of the criminal. Vito and Michael Corleone are the centers of consciousness within the newer film, and so return us to the "criminal as hero" conception of the original work. In fact, *The Godfather* goes one better than *Scarface* in that none of its represented lawmen have any ability to justifiably sustain the law. At least in the earlier film, the lawmen, although marginalized, were still capable of representing a system of justice. As already noted, in *The Godfather* we are asked to identify with an alternate system of law, with a code of honor that is specific to the needs of the Corleone family. This law is set against, and in many cases above, any outside law. In *The Godfather* we are set inside this familial law, looking out onto a corrupt world. And from this position we are not encouraged to make a moral judgment on the actions of the Corleone family.

Submerged Ethnicity

All that has been discussed thus far composes primarily the content of the films and exits on the epidermal surface of the works. These are elements of the script, as well as the mise en scène, the image, and the overall conceptualization – ones that are very much in evidence and that often present the overt intention of the film makers. What I would like now to explore is the notion of the submerged ethnicities, of alternate voices speaking through the film, and ones that are not always overtly apparent.

As Ella Shohat has noted, the questions that ethnic studies often overlook when describing representations of various ethnic groups are inquiries as to race, class, and gender. When investigated along these lines, the Italian-Americans in *The Godfather* take on a whole new dimension. It must be noted that in addition to representing Italian Americans, *The Godfather* presents us with a cinematic group made up of members who are predominantly *white, male,* and *upper class.* In terms of these later designations, the characters form a group much like the white, male Paramount executives who produced and distributed *The Godfather.* But the similarity between organized crime and business, especially as it is portrayed in the gangster film, is not a new insight and in fact represents one of the central metaphors of the genre. On the level of the films' making, however, I would like to explore the extent to which *The Godfather* may also incorporate a special wish or fantasy by an elite group, one that was then enthusiastically consumed by a predominantly white society.

This new way of looking at *The Godfather* is particularly useful when reexamining the notion of the family as a lost unit of love and protection in 1970s American society. It must be noted that what *The Godfather* presents us with is not only the image of white men working and warring together, but also the fantasy of that group as being a *homogeneous* ethnic entity. This group is made up almost exclusively of white Italian-American males, and not only is set at an earlier period in American history (a represented time from 1901 to 1959), but also is made up of individuals who live their lives according to the rules of a now fading memory of the old country. This particular construction of ethnicity then becomes especially significant when looked at in relationship to the historical period of the films' release. It must be noted that the early 1970s was an era in American history when white racial and ethnic purity was being seriously threatened by nonwhite peoples. During this period, America was about to emerge from a devastating war in Southeast Asia. (The United States pulled out of Vietnam in 1972 and finally signed a peace treaty in 1975.) At home, the United States was also embattled by pressing racial issues. Since the early 1960s, the Civil Rights movement had impacted strongly on American society, with African Americans demanding their place within many formerly all-white enclaves. Later in the 1960s, militants like Malcolm X or groups like the Black Panthers threatened white America's sense of security, a situation that was further shaken by the burning of inner-city ghettos. Against this backdrop, *The Godfather* must be seen as a significant fantasy, one that embodies the wish for an all-white militant group, one that exists to the exclusion of all other races and ethnic Americans. (Again, the wish here is for a time when organized crime could be controlled by one ethnic group, and is dramatized in the film by the active exclusion of African Americans, Puerto Ricans, and other ethnic groups in an antiseptic dream of racial and ethnic purity.)

It is also important to inquire about the specific dates that construct *The Godfather's* time frame. These dates are significant ones in American history, especially when considering America's relationships to other races or ethnicities. Both the Vito Corleone section which begins in 1917 and the later Michael Corleone section beginning in 1946 recall a time immediately after the United States' involvement in "just and honorable" wars, or at least in wars where America emerged as one of the triumphant victors. To set the film in the "before time," in a time before Vietnam, again underlines *The Godfather's* tendency for nostalgia, but now with the added understanding that it accomplishes a fantasy of purity as well. This is a time when American pride and moral purpose were intact. The final Michael sequence, however, was most notably set in 1958. This is an era again conveniently distinct from the period of American trauma – the 1960s – but also one desperately balanced at its doorstep. We are given a view of a time *just before* the assassination of JFK, the war in Vietnam, and the collapse of our cities.

The fantasy of control presented by *The Godfather*, then, seems to be an attempt to cover up a loss, but a loss, specifically, of what? As mentioned earlier, much is made in the article by John Hess (see note 21) that *The Godfather* actually accomplishes a critique of capitalism by its dramatization of the deterioration and loss of Michael's family. This loss, supposedly, leaves him a lonely and desolate man by the end of *Part II*. Perhaps so, but he *has* "gained the world" through his fantastic show of force, and to a capitalist society this is still a significant value. It must be remembered that in the last sequence of *The Godfather*, Michael has vanquished *all* of his enemies, an act that has left him the *one* most powerful man in American crime.

This is no small fantasy of power. The reality of this kind of power's being wielded by one man, however, either on the vast scale portrayed in the crime world of the film, in the real world of American big business, or on a more mundane level of the ordinary individual, is one that is steadily dwindling in our postmodern society. In intellectual circles, this situation has been touted as "the death of the subject," the death of individualism as such, and in everyday life it has been experienced as the individual's lessening ability to fully control or understand the world.[33] This last image of *The Godfather*, then – one in which Michael sits impassive and in close-up within the gigantic film frame – accomplishes the supreme fantasy of individual power. The wish now is for something that has been shaken, and perhaps is forever gone: the power and control of the singular, white, male subject. *The Godfather*, then, can be seen as an inflated wish for its reconstitution, and it has been the Italian-American criminal, with his connotation for a nostalgic form of power, that has been utilized to construct this fantasy.

THE GODFATHER PART III

The Godfather Part III (1990) appears nearly twenty years after the release of the two earlier films of the saga. This is a crucial distinction, one that impacts very strongly on the representation of ethnicity in the later film. *Part III* is a savvy work, and one that may at first seem exhausted in terms of the characters, images, and themes it represents. But because of the acknowledged position of *The Godfather* in film history, it can be assumed that Coppola was very aware of the cultural impact of the films he created, and of their status as sagas of an Italian-American family. For this reason, *Godfather III* can be seen as Coppola's attempted commentary on his own earlier work.

Godfather III is again a return, but this time its primary source of return is to the earlier *Godfather* films themselves. To facilitate this return, the film represents not only the work of the same director, but also of the same writer, Mario Puzo; the same director of photography, Gordon Willis; production designer, Dean Tavoularis; as well as the music of Nino Rota and Carmine Coppola. The reassembling of these talents, along with the inclusion of many of the same actors in their earlier roles, then, serves to create not only a continuation of *The Godfather* saga, but in many ways a *replication* of the earlier films.

To return to *The Godfather Part III* is to first return to the same visual and aural world. But here is our first clue, and also our first point of divergence. The visual world we return to is closer to that presented in *Part I* – the rich, warm environment of the mature Vito Corleone, one that had existed before the insidious demise of the family in the 1950s. This demise had visually been marked by the erosion of the sumptuous gold and brown tones of *Part I,* transforming them in *Part II* to the cold blues and steely grays (with a tinge of orange) of the Lake Tahoe and the Las Vegas 1958 settings. Now *Part III* begins with the image of the Lake Tahoe house in disrepair, abandoned and largely submerged under water, and presented to us on a cold, gray day recalling the one on which Michael murdered his own brother, Fredo.

This is a place of bad memories, of past sins. But to save us from this cold and destructive memory, *Part III* soon returns us to a Michael Corleone who is once again positioned in New York, in the same general location of his father's home. In many ways this home recreates the rich brown, black, and gold tones that were once in evidence, as well as thus recreating the familial sense of warmth of the original setting. In fact, almost the entirety of *Part III* is characterized by these colors, making a unified visual impression that recalls the opening sequence of *The Godfather Part I*. The haunting musical score similarly works to this end, especially the now-famous theme to *The Godfather* that begins the film and recurs throughout.

But aside from this visual evocation of the earlier *Godfather* films, *Part III* is not in itself a work of cultural nostalgia as I have argued for *Parts I and II*. The later film is a much more personal work with a new set of goals, and a new approach to its subject. Coppola's voice is very much in evidence here, commenting on his own past work, as well as on his own personal past. But interestingly, we, as the viewing audience, are an essential part of that past.

The film initially works as a kind of family reunion, a gathering of familiar and much loved characters after an absence of nearly twenty years. An early scene in the film introduces them to us again, and we marvel at how they've changed. But the deterioration or sadness that can be associated with the passage of time is not foregrounded here. Everyone looks very well, almost regal with their added years. (This includes not only Michael, Kay, and Connie, but also the woman who had once had a casual sexual encounter with Sonny in *Part I*. She is now the dignified mother of Sonny's illegitimate son, Vincent Mancini.) And all the children are now grown. Much attention is given to Sonny's Vincent Mancini, to Michael's own children Anthony and Mary, and even to Andrew Hagen, the now-priest son of Tom Hagen. And we, as viewers, almost form a large collective family with the Corleones. We are visiting with people whose past triumphs and sins we've witnessed, and whose children we've known from the time they were little – and even before.

This sense of the next generation is then continued in the quality of Italian Americans the film represents. Although the charm of the past may be in evidence, there is little that recalls the immigrant roots of the Corleone family, or any of the less appealing characteristics of their lower-, middle-, or even upper-class past. The Corleones are now "aristocracy." This reading is underlined by Michael's receiving of the Papal medal at the beginning of the film, a scene that recalls, albeit ironically, a knighting or even a coronation. The designation *Italian American* is thus transformed in this film, and is instead presented in association with all that is seemingly glorious and powerful about an Italian heritage. In *Godfather III*, Italy is presented as the land of the *signori* and their fabulous villas, of the wealthy northern Italian businessmen, of the great artists and composers, and of course, of the Vatican. Most importantly, Italy is now a place where crime is no longer petty or "of the people," but one maneuvered on the highest echelons of power. It must be added, however, that in this expanded arena Michael Corleone is associated with those components of Italian civilization that have traditionally been oppressors of the common people, especially the people of southern Italy. In fact, it was the landowners, the northern-based government, the aristocracy, and the Church itself that have been the historical exploiters of the southern peasantry (and the major contributors to the conditions in the late nineteenth and early twentieth centuries that caused the mass migration of southern Italians to the United States). In *Godfather III* Michael struggles to gain a controlling interset in the Immobiliare, the real estate holding company of the Vatican. By so doing, Michael comes full circle. As a landowner in association with northern businessmen and the Church, he becomes the symbolic exploiter of his own people. In a sense, he returns to the past, to the very causes of the formation of the original Mafia bands; but now he is on the wrong side. Michael's rise to power has dissociated him from his past, and from any possible ancient moral justification for his actions.

The sequence that significantly varies from this rendition of the "Italian" is the one that, unlike most of *Part III*, best recalls the gangster film sources of the saga. It takes place on the streets of Little Italy in New York City during an Italian festa. Like so much of *Godfather III*, this scene is fashioned to echo a memorable scene from an earlier *Godfather* work. This one recalls a similar festa, one set in the 1917 Vito Corleone section of *Part II*, a sequence in which Vito murdered Fanucci against the somber gaiety of the Little Italy celebration. The sequence, however, had ultimately meant to ennoble Vito and his acts of violence – acts, as we have noted, of displaced vengeance. Everything in that earlier sequence had been treated with respect, and with the bittersweet longing for a past time. In the segment from *Part III*, however, the respect is gone, as is any delusion of the nobility or glamour of this situation, either as a festival or as a rationale for a crime. Coppola uses this opportunity to demystify, as it were, the glamorization of the Mafia activity that he had constructed in the earlier works.

In this sequence, the Italian-American gangster is presented as a smarmy hood: either as Joey Zaza wolfing down a sausage sandwich and denying the existence of the "Mafia, Cosa Nostra, or whatever you want to call it," or even as the borderline Vinny Mancini who, now disguised as a cop, is nonetheless an edgy, brutal murderer. The violent encounter that follows results in an ugly confusion that endangers the lives of the innocent, even those of women and children. Here, both the villains and heroes are willing to sacrifice these once-to-be-protected individuals. The attack ends with no clear heroes and little honor. Zaza dies in an ugly and blood-splattered death (the death-in-the-street of the old-time gangster), and even the statue of the Madonna, the holy center of this procession, hits the pavement with a hollow thud.

Here, the Italian-American criminal is presented with condescension, and although we may laugh *at* these debased characters, there is none of the good-natured kidding, or the valor, of earlier gangster renditions. When compared to *Scarface*, it is interesting to note how the pairing of brutality with humor had somehow exalted the events, or at least distanced them so that they could be appreciated with transcendence. And in comparison with *The Godfather I* and *II*, we have noted how important honor was in relation to the represented acts. This scene in *Part III*, however, is unredeemed. With an attack masterminded by the unruly Vinny Mancini (and unauthorized by Michael, who understands that Zaza did not order the helicopter attack against him and his cronies), the scene is salvaged by neither humor nor valor.

But there *is* humor in *Part III*, and this is often uncharacteristically carried by Michael himself. Michael jokes and comports himself with casual goodwill. Twenty years have profoundly altered Michael's usual taciturn nature, a sometimes unsettling fact that is further complicated by his represented business standing. Here Michael's wealth and power are exaggerated to unheard-of proportions, a situation that occasionally threatens the fiction with its ludicrousness. As noted earlier, Michael and his now legitimate family are associated with Italian aristocratic settings, sprawling villas, expensive cars, majestic opera houses, and the Vatican itself. And then Michael, with all the kindliness of a patriarch dispensing Christmas candy, gleefully hands out gifts and payments of $100 million, $600 million, and even gifts of $50 million each to a roomful of Mafia heads. To embellish his cash gift to his associates, Michael then passes around a grab-bag of assorted fine jewelry. Michael's association with the acquisition of wealth and power is thus made more explicit than it was in either *Part I* or *II*. And although Michael's stated motivation is to become "legitimate" in business, his moral justification flounders in the face of his represented greed.

This inflated level of power is extended to Michael's ability to wield force. Michael dispatches his enemies in scenes that again echo earlier *Godfather* films. The most impressive in *Part III*, and the most reminiscent of the baptismal scene in *Part I*, is the intercutting between the majestic opera performance starring Michael's own son, and the murders Michael has ordered of his enemies. In this film, however, Michael is also the target of attacks by those enemies, as is the Pope himself. In this way, Michael's power and position are so great that he is, at least in this final way, equated with the Pope. The power and might that Michael had reached by the end of *Part II* is now seen as inflated to gargantuan proportions.

The film opens, however, with the statement, "Children are the only true wealth in this world." *Godfather Part III* is a film in which Michael seeks redemption. He seeks forgiveness for his sins, he promises God he will sin no more, he tries to become completely legitimate in business, and he tries to reunite his family. It must be noted that Michael fails at most of these goals, especially in that he forever destroys his Italian family and its future. In much the same way as the boy Vito Corleone had watched the murder of his mother in a Mafia-related instance, Michael witnesses the murder of his daughter, Mary. (Here the full connotation of this name should be acknowledged: Mary, the mother, the symbolic center of the family, and especially of young and future families.)

It is important to note that the role of Mary is played by Coppola's own daughter, Sofia Coppola, a choice that has received much unfavorable critical attention. The objections have been primarily to Sofia Coppola's weakness as an actress. In the scene where Mary is shot, however, the choice of his own daughter to play this role carries an emotional impact no other actress could have brought to the moment. Coppola had recently experienced the violent death of his own son, Gio. The desperate, soundless scream enacted by Al Pacino in response to Mary's death, one that symbolically strangles and deteriorates the man from whom it emanates, can best be seen as Coppola's own cry for his son.

The film ends with a scene that once again recalls an earlier one, now from *Godfather Part I*. Here, Michael Corleone, like his father Vito, dies quietly in his garden. This later scene, however, invites comparison to the original. In *Part I*, the ruthless Mafia Don had ironically died like an old-time Sicilian grandpa, peacefully playing among the tomato plants with his young grandson. Michael, on the other hand, dies desperately alone. Without grandchildren, Michael is seated on the arid and barren grounds of his Sicilian villa. The camera is kept in long shot during this sequence, underlining the impersonal, isolated, and unemotional quality of this death. Michael falls from his chair and rolls unceremoniously to the ground. Only a dog is there to nudge Michael's remains.

Godfather Part III has attempted in a number of ways to diffuse the myth of the Italian-American gangster as portrayed by the *Godfather Parts I* and *II*. *Part III* is a personal work that often elevates the codes for Italianicity to connote the most aristocratic and refined aspects of Italian culture, but ones also associated with the corrosive effects of power. The attempt here has been to remove, as much as possible, the honor and the legitimate use of violence by the Mafia. This has largely been done by rescinding the Sicilian rules of comportment for both men and women apparent in the earlier films. In *Part III* the characters are presented in such a way that they no longer embody the ways of "La Via Vecchia." Here the divergence from those old codes no longer functions to substantiate and legitimize the use of power. With the excuse of twenty years' passage, Michael is seen as a much broader character, one who is joking, convivial, and talkative, and then becoming violent when useful. We are no longer presented with the poles of control and release of action based on personal code of honor. In addition, the villains are not defined by their deviance from this code, by their inability to control their own passions, or by their lack of respect for women and for family. The motivation for most of the male characters in this film, including Michael, is purely for greed and power. This raw fact (a convention for the criminal of the early gangster films, and one *not* adhered to in either *Godfather I* or *II*) is here presented without the softening effects of false morality.

The same argument for a "submerged ethnicity," one that bespeaks the cultural bias of the additional makers of the film and of the viewing audience, and one that complements or even contradicts the surface reading of the film, is difficult to make here. A reason for this is the degree of control Coppola had over the final *Godfather* project, as well as the degree to which the question of ethnicity was consciously manipulated in the film. But perhaps the biggest deterrent to such a claim is the response from the viewing audience itself. This personal work had nowhere near the success of the first two films. In comparison, *Part III* was a box office failure. The attempt to deglorify the Italian-American gangster, to dismantle his honor, to show him in defeat, was not a popularly received message. The inflated fantasy of power presented in *The Godfather Part III* now actually ends (as Hess had claimed for *Part II*) with a man who has failed. Most importantly, this situation is not disguised or buffered by the healing effects of continued force. With Mary dead, Anthony an opera singer and definitively out of the family business, and Vinny an unlawful hothead, Michael and his family, as well as its code of honor, have ceased to survive.

In this way, *Part III* has been an attempt to destabilize the Godfather myth and its represented fantasy of power. Here the Italian American has been constructed to symbolize a force disconnected from its popular roots, and inflated to suggest gargantuan, even near-aristocratic proportions. The final effect of this inflation has been the demise of the individual and the destruction of his future. It must be noted that although *Part III* is set in 1979, the beginning of the Reagan era and the flamboyant rise of multinational capitalism, this is really a 1990s film bespeaking a rampant decentering of power and the further diminution of the individual.

In conclusion, it must be noted that the Italian American as criminal image in *The Godfather* films is neither, simply, an authentic fact nor a racial slur. It is, instead, an elaborate construction created by these films for the purpose of mass entertainment. This, however, does not altogether negate its racist roots. At the beginning of the twentieth century, the Italian immigrant was linked with crime by the Anglo-Saxon society and was feared as a stiletto-wielding Mafioso; in fact, the derisive term *dago* comes from *dagger*, the Italian's assumed weapon of choice. In the American film, this cultural prejudice has been incorporated for both ideological and utopian purposes. Different eras and works have rendered varying meanings to the notion of Italianicity. In *The Godfather I* and *II* the Italian is a construct that connotes pastness, a nostalgic category, one that ultimately serves to disguise a loss and to embody a wish for its reconstitution. The wish, as we have noted, is not only for the solidarity of the family, but also for a return to ethnic purity and to the lost power of the individual subject. In *Godfather III*, the Italian-American criminal image can no longer sustain a disguise for these losses. In all three *Godfather* films, then, the Italian American should not be seen as a realistic category and be judged in terms of his compliance to the "authentic" Italian-American experience, but a construct manipulated to engender an artistic and cultural effect.

NOTES

1. See, for example, L. Iorizzo and Salvatore Mondello, *The Italian-Americans* (Boston: Twayne Publishers, 1980), 184–215.
2. See, for example, Anthony L. LaRuffa, "Media Portrayals of Italian-Americans," in *Ethnic Groups* 4 (July 1982), 191–206.
3. John Cawelti, "The Mythology of Crime and Its Formulaic Embodiments," in *Adventure, Mystery, Romance* (Chicago and London: The University of Chicago Press, 1976), 51–79.

4. Roland Barthes, "The Rhetoric of the Image," in *Image, Music, Text* (New York: Hill and Wang, 1977), 31–51. Barthes uses the term *Italianicity* when describing the cultural connotations imbued in a photographic advertisement for "Panzani" spaghetti. Here Barthes notes how the message that these codes carry are dependent on the cultural knowledge of the reader.

5. Ella Shohat, "Ethnicities-in-Relation: Toward a Multicultural Reading of American Cinema," in *Unspeakable Images: Ethnicity and the American Cinema*, ed. Lester D. Friedman (Urbana and Chicago: University of Illinois Press, 1991), 215–250.

6. Ibid., 216.

7. Robert Stam, "Bakhtin Polyphony, and Ethnic and Racial Representation," in Friedman, 251–276.

8. Fredric Jameson, "Reification and Utopia in Mass Culture," in *Signatures of the Visible* (New York and London: Routledge, 1990), 34.

9. Fredric Homer, *Guns and Garlic: Myths and Realities in Organized Crime* (West Lafayette, IN: Purdue University Press, 1974), 3.

10. Cawelti, 78.

11. Carlos Clarens, *Crime Movies: From Griffith to the Godfather and Beyond* (New York and London: W. W. Norton & Co., 1980), 282.

12. Ibid.

13. Mario Puzo, *The Godfather Papers* (New York: G. P. Putnam and Sons, 1973), 32–69.

14. Robert K. Johnson, *Francis Ford Coppola* (Boston: Twayne Publishers, 1977), 95–106.

15. Peter Cowie, *Coppola* (New York: Charles Scribners Sons, 1989), 62.

16. Clarens, 53.

17. Ibid., 284.

18. Stam, 253.

19. Clarens, 87.

20. Ibid. Clarens reports that during the 1920s Capone was so popular that he had his own theatrical agent, William C. Grill. Capone had planned to appear in a fiction film and to donate his $200,000 salary from that performance to an unemployment fund. Although the Hays office put a stop to Capone's cinematic debut, he continued to receive an overwhelming flow of fan mail from his public.

21. John Hess, "*Godfather II*: A Deal Coppola Couldn't Refuse," in *Movies and Methods*, ed. Bill Nichols (Berkeley and Los Angeles: University of California Press, 1976), 23–30.

22. Cowie, 104.

23. Luigi Barzini, *The Italians* (New York: Atheneum, 1964), 252–275.

24. Richard Gambino, *Blood of My Blood: The Dilemma of Italian-Americans* (Garden City, NY: Doubleday, 1974), 5.

25. Ibid., 115.

26. Ibid., 115–145.

27. Ibid., 146–166.

28. Johnson, 112.
29. Francesco Cordasco, *Studies in Italian-American Social History* (Totowa, NJ: Rowan and Littlefield, 1975), 36.
30. Fredric Jameson, "Postmodernism and Consumer Society," in *The Anti-Aesthetic*, ed. Hal Foster (Port Townsend, WA: Bay Press, 1983), 111–125.
31. Cowie, 68.
32. Clarens, 277.
33. Jameson, 115.

BIBLIOGRAPHY

Affron, Mirella Jona. "The Italian-American in American Films 1918–1971," *Italian-Americana* 3 (Sring–Summer 1977), 233–255.
Barthes, Roland. "The Rhetoric of the Image," in *Image, Music, Text*. New York: Hill and Wang, 1977.
Barzini, Luigi. *The Italians*. New York: Atheneum, 1964.
Cawelti, John. "The Mythology of Crime and Its Formulaic Embodiments," in *Adventure Mystery, Romance*. Chicago and London: The University of Chicago Press, 1976.
Clarens, Carlos. *Crime Movies: From Griffith to the Godfather and Beyond*. New York and London: W. W. Norton & Co., 1980.
Cordasco, Francesco. *Studies in Italian-American Social History*. Totowa, NJ: Rowan and Littlefield, 1975.
Cowie, Peter. *Coppola*. New York: Charles Scribners' Sons, 1989.
Gallo, Patrick. *Old Bread, New Wine: A Portrait of Italian-Americans*. Chicago: Nelson Hall, 1981.
Gambino, Richard. *Blood of My Blood: The Dilemma of Italian-Americans*. Garden City, NY: Doubleday, 1974.
Garbee, John. *Gangsters from Little Caesar to the Godfather*. New York: Pyramid Publications, 1973.
Hess, John. "*Godfather II*: A Deal Coppola Couldn't Refuse," in *Movies and Methods*, ed. Bill Nichols. Berkeley and Los Angeles: University of California Press, 1976, 23–30.
Homer, Fredric. *Guns and Garlic: Myths and Realities of Organized Crime*. West Lafayette, IN: Purdue University Press, 1974.
Iorizzo, Luciano, and Salvatore Mondello. *The Italian-Americans*. Boston: Twayne Publishers, 1980.
Jameson, Fredic. "Reification and Utopia in Mass Culture," in *Signatures of the Visible*. New York and London: Routledge, 1990.
Jameson, Fredric. "Postmodernism and Consumer Society," in *The Anti-Aesthetic*, ed. Hal Foster. Port Townsend, WA: Bay Press, 1983, 111–125.
Johnson, Robert K. *Francis Ford Coppola*. Boston: Twayne Publishers, 1977.

Kolker, Robert Phillip. *A Cinema of Loneliness*. New York: Oxford University Press, 1980.

LaRuffa, Anthony L. "Media Portrayals of Italian-Americans," in *Ethnic Groups* 4 (July 1982), 191–206.

Mangione, Jarre, and Ben Morreale. *La Storia*. New York: Harper & Collins Publishers, 1992.

Puzo, Mario. *The Godfather Papers and Other Confessions*. New York: G.P. Putnam's Sons, 1973.

Pye, Michael, and Linda Myles. *The Movie Brats: How the Film Generation Took Over Hollywood*, New York: Holt, Reinhart, and Winston, 1979.

Shadoian, Jack. *Dreams and Dead Ends: The American Gangster/Crime Film*. Cambridge, MA and London, Eng.: MIT Press, 1977.

Shohat, Ella. "Ethnicities-in-Relations: Toward a Multicultural Reading of American Cinema," in *Unspeakable Images: Ethnicity and the American Cinema*, ed. Lester D. Friedman. Urbana and Chicago: University of Illinois Press, 1991.

Sollars, Werner. *Beyond Ethnicity: Consent and Dissent in American Culture*. New York: Oxford University Press, 1986.

Stam, Robert. "Bakhtin, Polyphony, and Ethnic Racial Representation," in *Unspeakable Images: Ethnicity and the American Cinema*, ed. Lester D. Friedman. Urbana and Chicago: University of Illinois Press, 1991.

Tomasi, Lydio. *Italian-Americans: New Perspective*. New York: Center for Immigration. Studies of New York, Inc., 1985.

Warshow, Robert. *The Immediate Experience*. New York: Doubleday, 1962.

Woll, Allen L., and Randall M. Miller, eds. *Ethnic and Racial Images in American Film and Television*. New York and London: Garland Publishing, Inc., 1987.

4 Ideology and Genre in the *Godfather* Films

IDEOLOGY AND THE GANGSTER GENRE

The gangster genre follows a pattern found in most Hollywood genres, the reinforcement of a prosocial ideology supportive of the status quo. To this end, it promotes adherence to law and order and the maintenance of a hierarchical social structure. The genre's basic structure buoys its ideology: the (usually) ethnic gangster rises from a poor working-class environment to social prominence through illegal and brutal means, only to slide back into destitution or fall to authorities or to a rival gang through his arrest or violent death. Several generic elements, however, complicate this ideological agenda. Foremost among them is the gangster's obvious appeal to his audience. The narration presents the gangster as a highly attractive figure, charismatic in his animal magnetism and in his physical and economic aggressiveness. He appeals to our sense of mayhem and license that would disrupt the social order, and his economic aggression is in the best American tradition of rugged individualism and laissez-faire capitalism. Therein lies the challenge to the genre's ideology, for in aping the corporate ways of American capitalism, the gangster exposes the ruthlessness and greed that undergird the American dream of material success.[1]

The conflicting prosocial and subversive elements within the gangster genre give rise to contradictions that cannot easily be explained away. Because of this, the gangster film often copes with these contradictions by deflection or simple solutions rather than by any attempt at real resolution. Generally speaking, the genre's discourse deflects from a telltale indictment of American capitalism by turning the narrative into a case of individual hubris and tragedy; it is the gangster who is evil in his overreach, in his breaking the bounds of restraint, and not a society that may be responsible for motivating an aggression for success at any cost. Instead, society acts as a savior, punishing the gangster and pinpointing his downfall as a moral that in the end recuperates him as well as the movie's audience from its enthrallment with his personality. The genre's ideology overrides, finally, the myth of the charismatic but outlawed individual and masks the contradictions that would undermine its apparent coherence.[2]

The gangster film employed a variety of strategies to sway its narrative to conservative conclusions and cloak its inherent contradictions until the mid-sixties when it briefly entered a progressive phase with *Bonnie and Clyde* in 1967 and *The Godfather* films in 1972 and 1974. The gangster films of the early 1930s – *Little Caesar* (1930), *The Public Enemy* (1931), and *Scarface* (1932) – defined the tension between the individual and society in a classic way. Because the films' narration focused on the character of the gangster himself and because of the strong, attractive personas of their actors, Edward G. Robinson, James Cagney, and Paul Muni, respectively, the gangster possessed a powerful appeal. To counteract this appeal, the discourse relied on both internal and external factors to diminish the gangster and recuperate the audience. Internal factors relate to character and plot. The gangster's hubris, his overweening pride and lust for power at all costs, operates as the cause for both his success and his downfall and not the rapacious capitalism that motivated his personal desires in the first place. The gangster's punishment and tragedy are therefore internally motivated, and his brutal death acts as a warning to all who would disturb the status quo. In addition, external factors such as prologues and epilogues reinforce the cautionary aspect of the narrative. Their insertion seems to have been motivated by the desire to police the sensationalism in Hollywood films before the enforcement of the Production Code which stipulated that crime could not be glorified. Prologues and epilogues to these three films crusade the message that the character depicted is a menacing social force that must be eradicated.

With the enforcement of the Production Code after 1933, gangster films diminished the tension between an attractive individual gangster figure and the need for a stable community by altering the narration's focus or by incorporating strong prosocial figures within the narrative to counteract the threat of the gangster. In *Hollywood Genres* (1981), Thomas Schatz describes three variations of the gangster film that appeared after 1933: the gangster as cop turned around, the Cain-and-Abel formula, and the middleman dilemma. Each strengthened the prosocial myth in various ways. The gangster-as-cop variation switched the focus of the narration from the gangster to the lawman who fought the gangster. The lawman figure assumed the tough, intelligent individualism of the gangster prototype in such films as *G-Men* (1935) and *Bullets or Ballots* (1936), with Cagney and Robinson, respectively, reversing their gangster roles of *The Public Enemy* and *Little Caesar*. The Cain-and-Abel formula pitted the gangster figure against an equally strong prosocial figure, whose values eventually held sway over the gangster's bad ways in such films as *Angels with Dirty Faces* (1938), with Cagney as the gangster and Pat O'Brien as his priest friend, and *Key Largo* (1948), with Robinson as the gangster and Humphrey Bogart as his antagonist. The middleman variation highlighted a person caught between prosocial and criminal forces, usually a criminal who decides to go straight but finds it difficult to shake off his past ties. Examples of this variation include *The Roaring Twenties* (1939) and *Kiss of Death* (1947), with Cagney and Victor Mature, respectively, as former criminals fighting off their pasts. Each variation continues to the nineties, as evidenced by *The Untouchables* (1987), whose hero Elliot Ness and his federal enforcers battle Al Capone and other

Prohibition gangsters; *A Bronx Story* (1994) in which Robert De Niro's father exerts a resolutely strong influence on his son to counteract the alluring influence of his son's gangster mentor; and *Carlito's Way* (1994), with Al Pacino as the reformed hood who wants to go straight, only to have his past interfere with his legitimate plans.

In the 1950s and early 1960s, two variations developed that did not significantly challenge the genre's ideology. The first was the development of a semidocumentary style with voiceover narration in such films as *The FBI Story* (1959), *Al Capone* (1959), and *The Rise and Fall of Legs Diamond* (1960). The authoritative voiceover provided the prosocial moral, and in the case of *Al Capone*, the narrator was the police figure responsible for the gangster's downfall. The other variation included gangster biographies that merely exploited the genre's melodramatic and violent elements: *Baby Face Nelson* (1957), *Machine Gun Kelly* (1958), *The Bonnie Parker Story* (1958), and *Pretty Boy Floyd* (1960).

Bonnie and Clyde reinvigorated the genre in the 1960s by challenging its ideology. In the 1967 Arthur Penn film, the myth of the charismatic gangster dominates over the myth of community and law and order. The film recaptured the charisma, flair, and powerful appeal of the gangster in Faye Dunaway's Bonnie Parker and Warren Beatty's Clyde Barrow, making them out to be heroes against the system. At the same time, the film depicted society or the system as economically cynical in its heartless response to the victims of the Great Depression. Clyde's "We rob banks" was a rallying cry for the destitute individual destroyed and betrayed by the system. The film restored the myth of the individual at odds with the system, but with no counteracting myth of the need for a stable, law-abiding society. The gangsters' deaths were not the elimination of threats to a stable society, but an eradication of vibrant personalities who lived in an aura of romance, imagination, drama, and passion. They were individuals who answered their audiences' own dreams of a larger-than-life stage beyond the conventional restrictions of the everyday – an attitude very much in the spirit of the late sixties, a time of radical upheaval encompassing the counterculture movement and the protest against Vietnam.

Despite subverting its genre's ideology, *Bonnie and Clyde* still could not rid the genre of its basic contradictions. The contradictions merely took an opposite slant. For example, though Bonnie and Clyde are rebels against the system in their robbing of banks, they may be viewed as as much a part of the system's capitalistic base as the banks themselves. One need only note Bonnie's enchantment with the "We're in the Money" sequence of *The Gold Diggers of 1933* to realize the robbers' complicity with the American dream of material success. Like the gangsters before them, Bonnie and Clyde both do and do not belong to the system. In addition, though their rebellion from a life of depression and boredom is an attractive affirming alternative, they also exhibit a wayward carelessness that suggests not only a subversive energy but one that is amoral as well.[3] In other words, *Bonnie and Clyde* contains the kinds of contradictions we find in gangster films before it, and like them, it disguises these contradictions. However, *Bonnie and Clyde* masks its contradictions by playing up the myth of the rebellious individual and not recuperating its subversion of the dominant ideology.

The Godfather films also significantly challenge the genre's dominant ideology, each film offering different challenges with quite different results. On the whole, the trilogy indicts American capitalism for the rampant materialism within society and subverts the dominant prosocial myth. However, each film offers its own complications to this agenda. *Part I*'s critique of the dominant ideology is more or less implicit rather than explicit, its largely classical discourse reworking in a complex way the tensions between the prosocial myth of the community and the myth of the lawless but attractive individual. *Part II*'s critique is the most explicit and uncomplicated of the three films, attacking the genre's ideology by drawing clear analogies between the Mafia and a capitalistic society in a highly reflexive narration. *Part III*'s critique expands on that of *Part II*, but its subversion is laced with irony as the myth of the family and the myth of the individual revive to complicate the triple condemnation of Michael Corleone, the Mafia, and society.

THE GODFATHER PART I (1972)

In "Reification and Utopia in Mass Culture" (1990), Fredric Jameson says that the ideological function in the first *Godfather* film is to disguise the economic cause at the heart of America's problems. For him, the Mafia acts as a displacement for American capitalism, a displacement that encourages us to believe that the cause for the deterioration of life in the United States today is not economic but ethical, not derived from a profit motive but from the mythic source of "the pure Evil of the Mafiosi" (32). However, this ideological agenda of the film runs into two complicating roadblocks. The first is the traditional one of gangster figures with whom we identify; the second is the subversive critique of America's capitalist base as the reason for the country's problems. The narration fully develops the first complication to the film's ideology as it subjectivizes the story of the Corleones' war with their enemies within the Mafia world by privileging the perspectives of Godfather Vito Corleone (Marlon Brando) and his heir, Michael (Al Pacino). Meanwhile, the narration implies the second complication to the film's ideology – its subversive critique – and prepares for its full-blown expression in *Part II*.

I would like to examine how the narration suggests these contradictory strands in the long wedding sequence at the film's start, strands that carry through to the end, ultimately defying any simple solution and recuperation. The wedding sequence clarifies the nature of the Corleone operation. On his daughter's wedding day, Vito Corleone honors requests from members of his extended family ("A don can never refuse a request on the day of his daughter's wedding"), requests that involve violence, bribery, and extortion. Moreover, as the wedding guests arrive, the FBI conducts a surveillance check of license plates in the parking lot outside the Corleone estate; meanwhile, another godfather, Barzini (Richard

Conte), confiscates a photo taken of him at the wedding by a photographer. Michael, who at the moment has dissociated himself from his family, tells his WASP girlfriend Kay (Diane Keaton) the story of how his father and Luca Brasi threatened a bandleader with death to force him to release Vito's godson Johnny Fontaine from his contract in order to further his career. Michael, a recent war hero, says to Kay, "That's my family, Kay, that's not me." The film constructs the myth of the Mafia as evil and sets up an immediate conflict between the Mafia and the law. (Note Sonny's [James Caan] confrontation with the FBI in the parking lot.) However, the narration also suggests that the Mafia's evil is society's evil as well, forming the analogy between the Mafia's corruption and the law itself. The first words on the soundtrack are the baker Bonasera's "I believe in America," a sentiment that changes to ambivalence in his request for vigilante justice to avenge his daughter's rape and beating because the American justice system failed to punish the guilty parties. This contradiction – I believe in America/I don't believe in its system of justice – represents the beginning of a progressive critique in the trilogy, one supported by the references to corrupt judges and politicians on the Corleone payroll as Vito dispenses instructions to his consigliere Tom Hagen (Robert Duvall) to handle the requests. But before the narrative can develop either the dominant ideology or the critique against it, the narration introduces two other elements that will further complicate its ideology – the myth of the individual and the myth of the family. The romanticization of Vito/Michael and the whole Corleone family deflects from the prosocial myth of the Mafia as evil and puts on hold the subversive myth of society as evil.

In the stunning opening take, the apparatus fades into an extreme close-up of Bonasera's face only to reveal that the true subject of the shot is Vito Corleone. A slow backward zoom settles just over the right shoulder of the Don as he sits listening to Bonasera's request. This elaborately formed over-the-shoulder shot is just one of several subjectivizing techniques that entices the viewer to identify with Vito and Michael. The wedding sequence revolves around

Vito's perspective, and though the film alternates between objective and subjective strategies in its classical omniscient narration, most of the subjective sequences focus on Vito or Michael. Several of these sequences utilize compelling subjectivizing techniques that reinforce the relationship between audience and character: the scene in which Michael suggests he meet with Sollozzo (Al Lettieri) and the police captain McCluskey (Sterling Hayden) ostensibly to negotiate, but really to kill them in vengeance for the attempted assassination on his father (slow zoom into an extreme close-up of Michael); the sequence detailing Michael's revenge (extreme close-ups, over-the-shoulder shots); Vito's meeting with the godfathers of the other five families to work out a truce (over-the-shoulder shot followed by a circling camera); and Vito's floundering collapse and death in his garden (unsteady hand-held camera). The narration's focus on Vito and Michael as the subjects of the narrative bolsters its development of the Corleone family as the good side in its conflict against the other Mafia families, a conflict that stems from Vito's refusal to enter the narcotics racket. The film concentrates on developing and resolving this conflict for most of its three hours, a preoccupation that overshadows, even counteracts, the prosocial myth of the Mafia as evil and stunts in its wake the implied critique of society.

The myth of the family or the film's romanticization of the Corleone unit reinforces the romantic myth of the central figures of Vito and Michael. The wedding sequence establishes the benevolent paternalism at the heart of the family myth, ritualized in Vito's role and actions as father to his immediate family and as Godfather to his extended family. Vito expresses the values that bind family members together in a warm, protective, patriarchal environment. He insists on allegiance, respect, loyalty, and reciprocity from Bonasera before granting him his request; he emphasizes the importance of faithfulness and interaction with family members in his advice to Johnny Fontaine, his godson; he exhibits paternal affection, dances proudly with his daughter, and refuses to take the family wedding picture until Michael shows up.

The myth of the family that Vito expresses provides another strand to the central narrative conflict, that of Michael's movement from voluntary outcast to Vito's heir, a movement that seals the symbiotic relationship between the two myths of family and individual that empower the Corleones.[4]

The contradictions that we find at the film's beginning complicate the ideology that the myth of the Mafia as evil would support. The tension that arises from the competing four myths – the Mafia as evil, society as evil, the romanticized individual, the romanticized family – give way in the long middle of the film to the individual, personalized conflict within the Mafia world that deflects from the larger social issues raised in the wedding sequence. However, the tension, which never really disappeared, surfaces and becomes palpable again at the end, beginning with the baptism sequence which Coppola purportedly intended to be ironic – revealing the hypocrisy of Michael, the family, and religion as the parallel editing cuts back and forth from the baptism (with Michael as godfather to his nephew) to the killings of the heads of the five families (which Michael ordered as Godfather). Coppola's intentions and the irony constructed by the apparatus through the discrepancy between Michael's "I do renounce Satan" and the brutal murders revive the myth of the Mafia as evil, but by this time, the audience has bought into Michael's fight for power to the extent that the reaction can only be mixed and complicated.[5] I would argue that it is the last sequence of the film that is more effective in shattering the romanticization of Michael, the scene in which Michael lies to his wife Kay about the murder of Carlo, the husband of his sister Connie (Talia Shire). What makes the ending effective in exposing Michael is the apparatus's construction of him as the object, not subject, of the sequence. Over-the-shoulder shots situate Kay as the subject, with Michael in the background under her scrutiny. Though Kay would believe Michael's lie that he did not order Carlo killed, the apparatus is successful in baring Michael's hypocrisy and heartlessness and prepares for its full-blown deromanticization of him in *Part II*.

THE GODFATHER PART II (1974)

Two quotations from interviews with Coppola reveal the critique of ideology that we find in *The Godfather Part II*. The first relates to the film's demythification of Michael and the family that we find in the second film:

> This time I really set out to destroy the family. Yet I wanted to destroy it in the way that I think is most profound – from the inside. And I wanted to punish Michael, but not in the obvious ways. At the end, he's prematurely old, almost syphilitic, like Dorian Gray. I don't think anyone in the theater can envy him. [Farber, "They Made Him Two Offers," 19]

The second quotation refers to the Mafia as a "metaphor for America":

> I always wanted to use the Mafia as a metaphor for America. If you look at the film, you see that it's focused that way. The first line is "I believe in America." I feel that the Mafia is an incredible metaphor for this country. Both are totally capitalistic phenomena and basically have a profit motive. [Farber, "Coppola and *The Godfather*," 223]

The deromanticization of Michael and the family goes hand in hand with the critique of capitalism implied by the second quotation. For one thing, a romanticized view of Michael and his family would continue to deflect from either a prosocial myth or a critique of that myth. The critique of American society as basically exploitative in motivation can only be made through the analogy between the Mafia, represented here by Michael and his family, and the capitalistic system. So the deconstruction of the latter follows upon the deconstruction of the former. In *Part II*, Michael is no longer empowered as an underdog individual endeavoring to maintain honor and gain power against the enemies of his family. He is seen for what he is – a high-class criminal. And the family no longer represents a utopian community; instead, it is in the process of disintegration.

Part II takes up the agenda of deromanticization begun at the end of the first film as it continues Kay's scrutiny of Michael and the apparatus's construction of him as object and not subject in the first long sequence of son Anthony's First Communion party at the Corleone estate on Lake Tahoe. While dancing with Michael, Kay reminds him of his promise to her seven years ago that the family business would be legitimate in five years. Later, Kay's role as chorus to Michael's illegitimacy climaxes after his visit to Cuba when she reveals to him that she aborted, not miscarried, their son: "Michael, you are blind; it wasn't a miscarriage; it was an abortion; just like our marriage is an abortion. I didn't want your son, Michael. This must all end." Meanwhile, the apparatus carries over its denial of subject status to Michael that we found at the end of *Part I*. At the beginning of *Part II*, it presents him first in a medium long shot as one set piece within the mise-en-scène of the party. In Michael's first business meeting during the party, the editing is shot-reverse-shot between him and Senator Geary, none of them an over-the-shoulder shot to establish a particular subject position. This contrasts directly to the opening shot of *Part I*, the over-the-shoulder shot from Vito's point of view, revealed by the slow zoom of the camera from the extreme close-up of Bonasera's face to a medium shot of the undertaker's whole figure. In *Part I*, Vito's paternal affection, sensitivity, and tact during business meetings and family engagements blurred the underlying ruthlessness and criminality of the family's activities and contributed to the romantic construction of the Corleones. In contrast, Michael's cold professionalism, bluntness, and bossy attitude bare the brutality that surfaces in his dealings with business associates and family members alike in *Part II*. The first sequence exposes the exploitative nature of Michael's relationships. His meeting with Senator Geary turns into an ugly confrontation, each extorting the other; he argues with Pentangeli, who distrusts Hyman Roth, over the mutually lucrative business deal with Roth's Jewish syndicate; he orders Connie to give up her lavish, loose lifestyle and to break her engagement with Merle, her new boyfriend; and his "agreeable" meeting with Roth's representative

Johnny Ola is tainted with hypocrisy since it is Johnny Ola, with Roth's approval, who has masterminded the upcoming attempt on Michael's life later that evening.

As the first sequence exposes the exploitation and manipulation that undergirds Michael's actions, it also signals the deconstruction of the family as a utopian unit. No longer do we find the warm secure relationships and traditional binding rituals that we saw at the beginning of *Part I*. At the start of *Part II*, Connie arrives with yet another fiancé in tow to ask Michael for more money to bankroll her loose lifestyle; her mother scolds her for neglecting her children; the orchestra puzzles over Pentangeli's request for the traditional Italian tarantella played at Connie's wedding in *Part I;* Fredo (John Cazale) can't prevent his alcoholic wife from making a scene on the dance floor; Pentangeli, who runs the Corleone business in New York, disagrees with Michael over sharing their turf with the Rosato brothers and doing business with Hyman Roth; and finally, Johnny Ola's and Hyman Roth's opportunity to assassinate Michael stems from Fredo's dissatisfaction over his secondary position in the family, having been passed over as successor to his father in favor of the younger Michael.

The demythification of Michael and the family in *Part II* finally makes possible the critique of ideology we find implied in *Part I* because now the critique of Michael/Mafia is the critique of capitalism as the cause for such organizations as the Mafia. *Part II* fulfills the potential for critique in *Part I* as it depicts the corruption of the gangster as part of a larger corruption that stems from the abuses within a system of free enterprise. The profit motive pervades all levels of society in the world of *The Godfather Part II*. It links public officials, legitimate businessmen, common hoods, and high-level Mafiosi. At the beginning of *Part II*, Michael reminds Senator Geary, "We're all part of the same hypocrisy, Senator." In the business deal with the Cuban dictator Batista, Michael and Hyman Roth are only two of many partners, who include U.S. senators, congressmen, and the heads of American conglomerates on the order of AT&T and U.S. Steel. In this business deal, the Corleones attempt to enter the mainstream of commerce that rein-

Fredo Corleone (John Cazale) asks his brother Michael (Al Pacino) for forgiveness. *The Godfather Part II* (1974), Copyright Paramount Pictures, 1974. Courtesy of the Museum of Modern Art Film Stills Archive

forces the analogy between them and capitalist America. This mainstreaming had already begun with Michael's marriage to the WASP Kay Adams, the family's investment in Las Vegas gambling, and the relocation of the Corleone home and headquarters to Nevada. The Corleone family is like any other family striving to attain the American dream of material success, but it achieves this success only through a series of compromises that destroy its integrity. The dangers inherent in the capitalist impulse surface in Michael's paranoid vengeance, exposing the worm at the heart of American society. Vito's "successful" separation of a personal family life of affectionate generosity and a professional life of criminal violence gives way to the inevitable collapsing of the personal and the professional in Michael's harsh treatment of the family in the name of economic power. The example of Michael gives the lie to the bourgeois notion that one can be virtuous in one's personal life yet ruthless in one's professional life, that the "goodness" of the one remains untouched by the viciousness of the other, all because ruthlessness is an accepted trait of the business ethic.[6]

Michael's confusion of the professional for the personal blinds him to the destruction he causes to the family structure. In *Part II*, he betrays those closest to him in his drive for absolute power. He orders the murder of his brother Fredo for Fredo's unwitting role in the attempted assassination on his life; he ostracizes Kay from her children because of her criticism and bitter disillusionment over his violent lifestyle; and he betrays Tom Hagen, the one person who remains faithful to him throughout, by questioning Tom's loyalty and cruelly suggesting that Tom accept other offers for his services if he can't agree with Michael's decision to unnecessarily eliminate all his enemies – "You gonna come along with me in these things I have to do or what? Because if you don't, you can take your wife, your family, and your mistress, and move them all to Las Vegas."

In contrast to *Part I*'s classic structure that chronicled Michael's rise to godfather status, *Part II* employs a reflexive parallel structure to chronicle Michael's corporate consolidation of power and his ruthless destruction of those who get in his way. The narration cuts back and forth between Michael's story in 1958–1959 (from the time of Anthony's First Communion to Fredo's killing) and Vito's story (from the time of his immigration to America at the age of nine in 1901 to his return to Sicily in 1925 to kill Don Ciccio, the person responsible for the deaths of his parents). The apparatus produces an analogous structure in its juxtaposition of the two generations. One effect of this is to reveal that the source of the corruption in Michael's generation lies in Vito's early life and that the diseases of a rampant capitalism not only extend through all levels of society, but span the entire first half of the twentieth century as well. The parallel structure makes clear the symbiotic relationship between Michael and his father: Vito's rise to power through crime not only parallels Michael's consolidation of power through crime, but also plants the seeds for Michael's moral failure in the later generation. Several of the early transitions between the Vito and Michael sequences reinforce this association through visual means provided by superimpositions and fades, which separate or unite the Michael and Vito figures, depending on their respective status in relation to each other. For example, in the second transition, Michael bids farewell to Anthony after the attempt on his life, his profile in close-up on the left of the screen; as the scene fades, the figure of the twenty-five-year-old Vito in 1917 appears on the right of the screen, leaning against a door frame watching his first son, Sonny. Though the fade and superimposition suggest a doubling, the figures are separate, since Vito, a grocer's assistant, is not yet involved in criminal activities. However, in the fourth transition, the fade and superimposition join the two figures as one blends into the other. Michael learns of Kay's "miscarriage" from Tom after his return from Cuba, his profile in close-up on the left of the screen; the superimposition places Vito on the same side of the screen over Michael's profile as he leans against the doorway watching his second son, Fredo, a newborn in 1919. The two figures are now one, as Vito has since joined a gang of petty thieves. Also, the sequence that follows chronicles Vito's assassination of Fanucci, catapulting him to the position of Godfather. The visual identification of Vito and Michael in the fourth transition not only implicates both but, more significantly, establishes the father's initiation into crime as the root of the son's condition and ultimate moral disintegration.

THE GODFATHER PART III (1990)

The mainstreaming of the Corleones in *Part II* represents the secularization of the ethnic Italian American of the Mafia myth. Jameson calls this the Corleones' "fall into history." Jameson is referring to the myth of the Mafia as evil and the utopian myth of the family portrayed in *Part I*. He argues that *Part II* deconstructs those myths as the mythic content of *Part I* falls into history itself. The mafiosi actually turn into mainstream businessmen in their attempt to invest in legitimate schemes with the

Batista government along with other U.S. corporations and political figures. Meanwhile, *Part II* undercuts the utopian benevolent paternalism of the family in *Part I* by tracing its roots back to feudal Sicily and showing that its survival depends on "forms of repression and sexism and violence" (34). Jameson's thesis depends on the ideological function of *Part I* to disguise the economic cause of America's problems by constructing the Mafia as a displacement for American capitalism. However, this prosocial rendering of the Mafia as evil is itself undercut by the romantic myths of the individual and the family in *Part I*. To fully appreciate Jameson's thesis, one must include Michael in the "fall into history" as a necessary movement toward an association of the Mafia with American capitalism. The deromanticized Michael in *Part II*, then, is an "ordinary" businessman, corrupt and corrupting, like the judges, lawyers, journalists, police, and politicians such as Senator Geary that the Corleones have on their payroll.

Part III of the *Godfather* trilogy, made sixteen years after the second film, continues the fall from myth into history, from mystification into critique. The movie completes the process of Michael's transformation from mafioso to legitimate businessman when he sells his gambling investments and buys into a European conglomerate, International Immobliare. Michael's secularization fulfills the critique of capitalism, since he discovers that the world of legitimate business is just as corrupt as the Mafia's, forcing him to resort to the same ruthlessness and violence in order to survive and be successful in the "real" world. Immobliare is capitalism on a global scale, implicating religious as well as national institutions. Archbishop Gilday, the Pope's financial advisor, is a main player in the Immobliare scheme, acting as a go-between for Michael and the corporation. The movie even implicates the death of Pope John Paul I in 1979 as part of a plot to gain control of the company.

Part III's "fall into history" is complicated by an attempt to resuscitate the myths of the individual and the family, but as much as these two myths undercut both the prosocial myth and its critique in *Part I*, so the subversive critique of capitalism in *Part III* nips any stirrings that the family may regain its utopian unity or that Michael may redeem himself to his critics and audience. For one thing, Michael's attempts to redeem himself by achieving full legitimacy backfire, since the description of "legitimacy" proves a euphemism in a corrupt national and global corporate environment. Michael merely moves into a larger arena of which he has been a part all along. But the attempt to rejuvenate the family and to seek redemption seems genuine on Michael's part. At the beginning of *Part III*, he has moved the family back to its roots in New York City; he revives the family's relationship with the church by contributing $100 million to a Sicilian fund for the needy, receiving in return the medal of San Sebastian; at the reception after the religious ceremony, Connie leads the orchestra and guests in the singing of the traditional Italian tarantella played at her own wedding in *Part I;* Michael craves family gatherings and togetherness, asking Anthony and Mary (Sofia Coppola) to include their mother in the Corleone parties; he is flexible in allowing Anthony to pursue a singing career; he agonizes over the murder of Fredo and confesses his sins to Cardinal Lamberto (Raf Vallone); he even confesses his transgressions to Kay and asks for her forgiveness; he takes in Sonny's bastard son, Vinnie (Andy Garcia), and trains him to take his own place as Godfather; and Connie assumes a powerful role as an unofficial godmother.

The family, though broken, shows strong signs of coming together at the same time that Michael becomes legitimate and also sensitive to his past heartlessness. However, Michael and the family cannot overcome the consequences of their past actions and the world that overwhelms them. Michael is overwhelmed necessarily by the consequences of his earlier crimes and sins; it shows in his physical deterioration. And his attempt to legitimatize destroys, ironically, any desired family unity and redemption. In selling off the Corleone business to other mafiosi, Michael incurs the wrath of Joey Zaza (Joe Mantegna) and is pulled back into the intrigue and violence of the gangsters. In maneuvering to control International Immobiliare through his purchase of the majority of its stocks, he invites the disfavor of its board, headed by Lucchesi, who plots to regain control by delaying tactics, betrayal, and assassination. Try as he may, Michael cannot extricate himself and the family from the web of destruction woven in the past. The fatal shooting of his daughter Mary when he was the intended victim ruins Michael's desire for family unity and forgiveness for his past deeds from Kay, his former wife, and still chorus to his moral failure.

In my analysis of genre and ideology in *The Godfather* trilogy, I have been arguing emphasis rather than exclusivity. The tensions that inhere in the trilogy given the prosocial myth, the myth of the individual, the myth of the family, and the critique of ideology surface in varying degrees throughout all three films. The critique of ideology may override the other three myths in *Part II* and *Part III*, but Michael's moral isolation at the end of *II* and the tragic death of his daughter Mary at the end of *III* may be construed as society's revenge for the crimes of his life and therefore as part of the prosocial strain within the trilogy. And though *Part II* upsets the romance of Michael's character, it includes the romance of Vito as a young man who rises successfully to godfather status in the Little Italy of the new world in the early part of the century. The apparatus emphasizes the contrast between the critique of Michael and the romance of Vito by constructing different styles to present their stories. The sharp pictorial realism of the present of Michael's story contrasts with the soft-focus nostalgia of Vito's early history. Also, in *Part III*, though Michael's attempt at redemption fails in the face of the withering critique of the capitalist venture, his nephew Vinnie's actions to secure a place in the family and as probable heir to Michael recall the heroic gumption and grace we associate with the young Michael of *Part I* and the young Vito of *Part II*. In other words, though I have argued emphasis in each of the films, the complications that accompany the challenge to ideology in the trilogy caution a view of lines drawn clearly or conveniently given one's preference for any given mythic construction. I would argue instead that the trilogy provides no clear statement in the tug of its conflicting elements. What it does provide clearly is a challenge to ideology that

The aging Godfather (Al Pacino) and the Godfather in waiting (Andy Garcia), *The Godfather Part III* (1990), Copyright Paramount Pictures, 1974. Courtesy of Jerry Ohlingers Movie Material Store

complicates any simple solution to the tensions underlying the genre of which it is a part.

THE GODFATHER TRILOGY AS A PROGRESSIVE FILM

The first two films of *The Godfather* trilogy hit the screens in 1972 and 1974, respectively, during a period in American history darkened by the unpopular Vietnam War and by the scandal of Watergate. Distrust of the government during the Vietnam War turned into cynicism and disillusionment during the Nixon years. It is no wonder that *The Godfather* films would include a critique of the American system during this time of social upheaval and dimming faith in the country's traditional values. The two films were part of a cluster of radical films made during the period that disrupted the mainstream ideology of the Hollywood film and its genres. In addition to *Bonnie and Clyde,* such films as *The Graduate, McCabe and Mrs. Miller, Chinatown, Five Easy Pieces, Lenny,*

Nashville, and *Taxi Driver* undermined traditional myths without recuperating them. Such films fit into the mold defined by Barbara Klinger as the "progressive film." Klinger takes her cue from Jean Louis Comolli and Jean Narboni in their landmark *Cahiers du Cinema* article "Cinema/Ideology/Criticism" in which they define categories of films in relation to their support or critique of ideology on both the levels of subject matter and discourse. The category that is most relevant here is the "e" category made up of Hollywood films that are basically conservative but contain radical elements that disrupt the text. In many cases, these radical elements are recuperated or glossed over by simple and easy solutions. However, an extreme "e" film will resist a successful recuperation of its radical elements so that the disturbance to the dominant discourse and ideology remains at the end (687). Klinger follows this up by further categorizing extreme "e" films as a "progressive genre" that produces an "alternative or 'countercinemas' within the province of dominant cinematic practice": "Difference from the environment of conventions within which these films exist, then, is a paramount feature of their progressive status, and the rationale by which they are accorded a radical valence" (79). *The Godfather* trilogy is a primary example of a progressive film. *Part I* plays up the tensions between a prosocial myth and the myth of the romanticized gangster, never quite resolving the conflict between the two, whereas the other two films pursue a relentless critique of American capitalism and the American dream. Furthermore, *Part II* utilizes a narration that is more modernist than classical, stressing theme and character study through an analogous parallel structure. The radical elements in the trilogy operate on the levels of both content and discourse, and the narration never recuperates the critique of capitalism in *II* and *III.*

One way to understand more completely the progressive nature of *The Godfather* trilogy is to compare it with the 1945 film it refers to in its text, *The Bells of St. Mary's.* The reference to *The Bells of St. Mary's* occurs early in the film, just after the assassination attempt on Vito's life, which takes place during the Christmas holidays of 1945. Michael discovers that his father has been shot through a newspaper headline on the street fronting Radio City Music Hall where the marquee advertises *The Bells of St. Mary's,* which was a big hit during the Christmas season following the end of World War II. *The Bells of St. Mary's* is a good example of an "e" film whose narrative includes radical elements only to recuperate them in the end. Ingrid Bergman's Sister Benedict is the radical element that threatens to undermine the film's ideology as she challenges the authority of the patriarchal Father O'Malley (Bing Crosby). Father O'Malley rebuffs each challenge, and the narrative glosses over complex issues by recuperating Sister Benedict to the priest's way of thinking in a film that ultimately celebrates traditional family values and a capitalism sugared over as benevolent paternalism.[7]

The Godfather trilogy, which unsettles the dominant ideology to the extent that it resists recuperation, is a stark contrast to the 1945 film it refers to in its text. Unlike *The Bells of St. Mary's,* the trilogy undermines wholesome family relationships, attacks the capitalistic base within American society as malevolent aggression, and rejects any simple solution to complex problems such as Michael's ill-fated attempts at legitimacy and family reconciliations in *Part III.* The sequence in which *Part I* includes *The Bells of St. Mary's* analogizes the contrast between the trilogy and the Bergman/Crosby vehicle. The stark reality of Vito's assassination frames the reference to the romanticized and sentimental McCarey film. After Sollozzo's thugs shoot Vito on the street, the apparatus cuts to a long shot of Radio City Music Hall where *The Bells of St. Mary's* is playing, then cuts to Michael and Kay coming out of the theater with the movie's title song on the soundtrack. Kay asks Michael, "Mike, would you like me better if I were a nun, like in the story, you know?" Michael answers, "No." Kays then asks, "Well, would you like me better if I were Ingrid Bergman?" to which Michael responds, "Well now that's a thought!" Kay stops with a serious look on her face; misinterpreting her, Michael says, "No, I would not like you better if you were Ingrid Bergman." Kay wails, "Michael, Michael," and leads him to the newspaper stand on the street and to the headlines, "Vito Corleone Feared Murdered." As Michael crosses the street to get to a phone, a car horn blares the change of mood as it disrupts the "Bells of St. Mary's" song on the soundtrack, signaling the return of the plaintive *Godfather* theme as Michael rushes into the phone booth. Michael's transition occurs at this crucial juncture between fantasy and reality, between imagining Kay as Ingrid Bergman from *The Bells of St. Mary's* and reading the screaming headlines announcing his father's shooting. Up to this point, he has resisted the family business and escaped its troubled status within society; now, he takes the plunge into the complicated generic gangster world of *The Godfather,* protecting his father in the hospital and killing Sollozzo and McCluskey in vengeance.

At this turn in the narrative, the figure of Michael inscribes the complex outlines of the challenge to the genre's ideology. He is, at one and the same time, the film's heroic subject defending the family's honor and the perpetrator of a capitalistic ruthlessness inherent in the American system. Michael's actions in *Part I* appeal to our fantasy of the underdog gunman, but they possess the seeds that will doom him to fragmentation and isolation, a status realized in the final images of the other two films in the trilogy: at the end of *Part II,* Michael is at the apex of his power, the king-of-the-hill American gangster, but he sits all by himself, withdrawn and expressionless, huddled against the cold autumn bareness of his Lake Tahoe estate; and at the end of *Part III,* years after the death of his daughter Mary, Michael is in a state of decline, an old, decrepit, guilt-ridden American businessman, sitting alone in the broiling sun, slumped in a posture that may be sleep but suggests the deep repose of death.

NOTES

1. For commentary on the contradictions that we find in the gangster film, see Thomas Schatz, *Hollywood Genres: Formulas, Filmmaking, and the Studio System* (New York: Random House, 1981), 81–95; Jack Shadoian, *Dreams and Dead Ends: The American Gangster/Crime Film* (Cambridge, MA: MIT Press, 1977), 5; and Robert Warshow, "The Gangster as Tragic Hero," in *The Immediate Experience* (New York: Atheneum, 1971), 127–133.

2. See Judith Hess Wright, "Genre Films and the Status Quo," in *Film*

Genre Reader, ed. Barry Keith Grant (Austin: University of Texas Press, 1986), 41–49, for an incisive argument on the strategies that Hollywood genres use to resolve contradictions. Her discussion includes the Western, the science fiction, the horror, and the gangster genres.

3. For more on *Bonnie and Clyde*'s inversion of generic expectation and the complications to ideology that it yields, see John G. Cawelti, "*Chinatown* and Generic Transformation in Recent American Films," in *Film Theory and Criticism,* 4th ed., ed. Gerald Mast et al. (New York: Oxford University Press, 1992), 508; and Robin Wood, *Arthur Penn* (New York: Frederick A. Praeger, 1970), 75.

4. Fredric Jameson views the first film's myth of the family as having a utopian function in the society of the 1970s; it provides the fantasy of an integrated community formed by patriarchal and authoritarian bonds for an audience given over to social fragmentation and atomization. See "Reification and Utopia in Mass Culture," in *Signatures of the Visible* (New York: Routledge, 1990), 34.

5. See Stephen Farber, "Coppola and *The Godfather,*" *Sight and Sound* 41:4 (Autumn 1972), 223, for a report on Coppola's intended irony in the parallel montage of the baptism/killings sequence.

6. In "Coppola and *The Godfather,*" Farber observes that this accepted division in American life represents a confusion of values, an assumption that there is "no correlation between what a man is personally and what he may be forced to do in his work . . . trading the Judeo-Christian ethic for jungle ethics when the dollar is at stake" (218).

7. For a further discussion of recuperation in Hollywood films, see Robin Wood's "Ideology, Genre, Auteur," in *Film Theory and Criticism,* 4th ed., ed. Gerald Mast et al. (New York: Oxford University Press, 1992), 475–485, in which he looks at two other Hollywood films of the 1940s, one that recuperates its subversive elements and another that resists recuperation – *It's A Wonderful Life* (1946) and *Shadow of a Doubt* (1943), respectively.

BIBLIOGRAPHY

Cawelti, John G. "*Chinatown* and Generic Transformation in Recent American Films," in *Film Theory and Criticism,* 4th ed., ed. Gerald Mast, Marshall Cohen, and Leo Braudy. New York: Oxford University Press, 1992, 498–511.

Comolli, Jean-Louis and Jean Narboni. "Cinema/Ideology/Criticism," in *Film Theory and Criticism,* 4th ed., ed Gerald Mast, Marshall Cohen, and Leo Braudy. New York: Oxford University Press, 1992, 682–689.

Farber, Stephen. "Coppola and *The Godfather,*" *Sight and Sound* 41(4) (Autumn 1972), 217–223.

"They Made Him Two Offers He Couldn't Refuse," *New York Times* (22 December 1974), Section 2, 1, 19.

Jameson, Fredric. "Reification and Utopia in Mass Culture," in *Signatures of the Visible*. New York: Routledge, 1990, 9–34.

Klinger, Barbara. "'Cinema/Ideology/Criticism' Revisited: The Progressive Genre," in *Film Genre Reader*, ed. Barry Keith Grant. Austin: University of Texas Press, 1988, 74–90.

Schatz, Thomas. *Hollywood Genres: Formulas, Filmmaking, and the Studio System*. New York: Random House, 1981.

Shadoian, Jack. *Dreams and Dead Ends: The American Gangster/Crime Film*. Cambridge, MA, and London: MIT Press, 1977.

Warshow, Robert. "The Gangster as Tragic Hero," in *The Immediate Experience*. New York: Atheneum, 1971, 127–133.

Wood, Robin. *Arthur Penn*. New York: Frederick A. Praeger, 1970.

"Ideology, Genre, Auteur," in *Film Theory and Criticism*, 4th ed., ed. Gerald Mast, Marshall Cohen, and Leo Braudy. New York: Oxford University Press, 1992, 475–485.

Wright, Judith Hess. "Genre Films and the Status Quo," in *Film Genre Reader*, ed. Barry Keith Grant. Austin: University of Texas Press, 1986, 41–49.

5 Family Ceremonies: or, Opera in *The Godfather* Trilogy

If the concluding sequences of *Godfather III* bring the epic saga of the Corleone family to a tragic end, they also represent the most dramatic culmination of what is, certainly, one of the underlying impulses of the *Godfather* films: that is, their operatic cast. As if to underscore the role played by opera throughout the films, Mary Corleone is shot to death on the steps of the Teatro Massimo Opera House in Palermo after a long sequence set within the opera house itself. In the course of this sequence, Mary and her parents, Michael and Kay Corleone, witness a performance of Pietro Mascagni's 1890 operatic work, *Cavalleria Rusticana*, in which the Corleone son, Anthony, sings a leading role. Intercut with actions taking place within and without the opera house, scenes of Mascagni's opera provide *mise en abime* for critical moments of the film even as they go to the core of Coppola's esthetic.

Important as they may be, scenes of actual opera houses or performances constitute, as I hope to show, but one aspect – albeit the most explicit – of the love for opera that gives Coppola's work a special resonance. The influence, in particular, of two Italian composers of the previous century – that is, of Mascagni himself and of Verdi – is felt not only in this sequence but throughout the trilogy. Clearly influenced by romantic and verist Italian opera of the past century, Coppola may also owe a debt to two of the most "operatic" of Italian film makers: that is, Luchino Visconti and Bernardo Bertolucci. (In addition to directing films, Visconti also produced and staged both plays and operas.) Indeed, the scene in *Godfather III* that is staged within the opera house brings to mind memorable scenes in films by Visconti and Bertolucci. As in *Godfather III*, such scenes suggest parallels with events and passions taking place offstage even as they offer a dramatic backdrop for conspiracies and intrigues. In this sense, they confirm Catherine Clement's observation that "opera is the place for intrigues, love affairs, glances that intersect and never meet" (Clement, 4). Thus, in Visconti's 1954 film, *Senso,* a film set in the era of Italian unification, a performance of Verdi's *Il Trovatore* prompts the audience to react with nationalistic fervor and to shower the performers with bouquets with the colors of the new Italy about to be born; the protagonist of Bertolucci's *The Spider's Stratagem* (*La strategia del ragno,* 1970) discovers the identity of the men who murdered his father – as well as his father's true identity – in the same opera house where his father was assassinated.

Although music plays as vital a role in these films as it does in the *Godfather* trilogy, they all lack, it is true, what is no doubt *the* single defining characteristic of opera – that is, the presence of beautiful voices that express the most extreme of human passions. In this respect, however, one must remember that, in opera, voices are part of a complex spectacle that is at once highly visual and self-consciously theatrical. Underscoring the dramatic, ceremonial nature of the operatic spectacle, poet W. H. Auden observed that "its pure artifice renders opera the ideal dramatic medium for a tragic myth" (Auden, 469). As for opera's visual dimension, French critic Michel Poizat reminds us that "no stage presentation draws more heavily on its visual elements than opera. The various devices of mise-en-scène such as costumes and scenery, complex, mechanically driven special effects, and visual illusions such as trompe l'oeil and perspective have been fundamental in opera since its beginnings in the seventeenth century. It should not be forgotten that opera as we know it was born with the baroque period, an era with a penchant for trompe l'oeil and perspective effects" (Poizat, 32).

There is no doubt – and I would like to return to this in connection with Coppola's debt to Mascagni – that the *Godfather* films share the taste for dramatic "artifice" and striking visual effects that critics such as Auden and Poizat discern in opera. But first I think it is important to note that Coppola emphasizes the theatricality and ceremonial nature of the *Godfather* films largely through certain formal strategies associated with opera. Indeed, two formal strategies in particular are as fundamental to the *Godfather* films as they are to most operas. For Coppola makes great use both of choral elements – or, more precisely, of the alternation of choral scenes with those focused on two or three characters – and of recurring motifs and themes. In operatic works both these strategies play a role that is often interconnected and frequently multifaceted – that is, it may involve dramatic structure and narrative as well as themes. For example, choral moments conventionally serve a role that is both narrative (as exposition) and structural (for dramatic emphasis).

Discussing, for example, the juxtaposition of ensemble (or choral) numbers with arias and duets, in a pioneering work devoted to the dramatic aspects of opera, Joseph Kerman observes that ensembles were conventionally "employed for the beginning of acts, where vivid exposition was needed, and particularly at the ends of acts, where the plot reached its maximum complexity and brilliance" (Kerman, 73). As for repetitions, like the presence of the chorus at the end of an act, they, too, heighten the "complexity" and "brilliance" of the action. For, whether visual or aural, each time that a motif is repeated, it assumes new force. That is, each successive echo or refrain imprints itself more strongly upon our sensibility than the preceding ones since it resonates with what we have already seen or heard. Each repetition triggers what Kerman calls "imaginative reminiscence." Speaking of repeated themes in Verdi, in particular, Kerman writes that "the music is used for imaginative reminiscence and almost always in some climactic context" (Kerman, 132). Forcing us to view, to measure, the present through the lens of the past, these repetitions create, perhaps, a sense of inevitability even as they contribute to the impression of flow and continuity that inheres to the work as a whole. "Recurring themes," writes Kerman, "force the listener to relate one moment in the drama to another, force him to think past rigid boundaries between numbers, they are truly continuous in effect" (Kerman, 131).

Turning from opera to film, it is clear that both these impulses are as vital to the *Godfather* trilogy as they are to, say, Verdi. Although, in certain respects, operatic motifs and strategies become more marked with each successive *Godfather* film – culminating, as suggested earlier, in the concluding scenes of *Godfather III* – these two impulses are visible virtually from the very first: that is, in the initial wedding scene that opens *The Godfather*. Like the conventional opening chorus of many operas, this scene is marked by pageantry, pomp, and spectacle: the orchestra plays, wedding guests dance, songs are performed by guests and members of the Corleone family. Pointing to the film's theatrical cast, this scene is also the first embodiment of the dramatic visual and moral contrasts that will punctuate the film. Coppola repeatedly takes us from the glittering, sunlight scenes of outdoor festivities to the Don's shuttered study where hushed dramas of power unfold. At the same time, this scene also plays the expository role that often falls to opening operatic choruses. Going from ensemble shots to scenes focused on several individuals, it introduces us to the various members of the family: in rapid strokes, Coppola paints Michael's ambivalence about the family "business," Sonny's impetuousness, the greed of Connie's new husband. So, too, does it reveal much about the defining characteristics, the ethos, of this Sicilian clan. Theirs is a patriarchal world based on honor and tradition, a world that prizes family and children. His is an auspicious day for those who have come to ask a favor of Don Vito, for, we are told, no Sicilian can refuse a request made on the day of his daughter's wedding.

There is still another aspect, moreoever, to the opening "chorus" of *The Godfather*. But it is one that will become clear only in retrospect. For this scene also announces many of the aural and visual motifs that will be repeated, and will gather strength, as the film (and, indeed, the trilogy) progresses. The best known of these is undoubtedly the *Godfather* musical theme which concludes the

Ceremonies: The wedding of Connie from *The Godfather* (1972), Copyright Paramount Pictures, 1972. Courtesy of the Museum of Modern Art Film Stills Archive

wedding sequence as the Don sweeps his daughter into his arms for a dance. But it is only one motif among many. Triggering what Kerman calls "imaginative reminiscence," each time we hear or see these motifs they will remind us – like the repeated themes of an opera – of scenes, actions, emotions witnessed earlier. Thus, for example, throughout the film, the family "business," the dealings of power, will be associated with images seen in the opening sequence: images of dark-suited men in enclosed rooms, of gestures of deference and power. Creating a powerful subtext of their own, these images will remain with us long after the words that were actually spoken in this sequence have faded from memory.

Even as these repetitions imprint themselves on our minds and senses, they also serve – and here, too, the analogy with opera is compelling – a thematic role. That is, by constantly reminding us of earlier scenes, they give rise to an insistent comparison between past and present. This persistent sense of the past gives an epic dimension to the film even as it underscores what is perhaps the most fundamental theme of the trilogy: the wrenching contrast between the family's rise to wealth and power and its inner decline. Thus, the initial wedding scene, in which the family is united and peaceful, becomes a kind of standard by which we judge, and lament, the growing decay of family bonds seen at each successive reunion. One has only to compare, for example, the wedding scene of *Godfather I* with a similar scene that occurs near the beginning of *Godfather II* – in which the family is celebrating the First Communion of Michael's son (and Vito's grandson) Anthony – to see how powerfully such repetitions function. For spectators who have not seen or cannot remember *The Godfather*, this sequence acts only as an introduction (albeit a masterful one) to *Godfather II*. Like the initial wedding scene, it too functions as a choral moment – filled with dance and music – of exposition. But for those who remember scenes of Connie's wedding in *The Godfather*, and who are thus subject to "imaginative reminiscence," this sequence takes on a much deeper resonance. Memories of an earlier time underscore not only the family's rise to immense power and wealth but also its inner rot. Senators may be at their beck and call, but the bonds of family love and duty are disintegrating: Fredo, married to a blonde floozy, drinks; Connie ignores her children as she flits from one husband to another; Michael neither feels nor inspires the love for family that governed his father's life. Indeed, the implicit comparison between this scene and the remembered sequence of *The Godfather* suggests that the use of recurring motifs play a role analogous to that of the many flashbacks that punctuate *Godfather II*. No less than every flashback, each repetition underscores the lacerating contrast – at the heart of the film – between past and present.

If the family rituals set the stage for recurring themes, so too do they highlight the ceremonial dimension of the films. Like the choral moments that conventionally mark the beginnings and ends of operas or operatic acts, these rituals too are often used to

Ceremonies: Anthony's First Communion, with his parents (Al Pacino and Diane Keaton), *The Godfather Part II* (1974), Copyright Paramount Pictures, 1974. Courtesy of the Museum of Modern Art Film Stills Archive

mark beginnings and endings even as they create the sense that we are watching a theatrical ceremony or ritual. For example, the initial wedding scene of *The Godfather* is matched, toward the end, by a baptism. At the same time, the various performances that often take place during these ritual gatherings – for example, the songs and dances performed at the wedding – further heighten the sense of spectacle that clings to these scenes and, indeed, to the film as a whole.

The ceremonial cast of the *Godfather* films has, moreover, still another dimension. It is one that extends beyond the family rituals, beyond the many performances that remind us that we are watching one more spectacle. For it seems to me that ceremony is most in evidence, and most significant, not when it comes to family rituals like weddings but, instead, to family "business": that is, to violence. And it is here, I would argue – that is, in respect to the ceremonial cast assumed by violence – that one begins to sense the debt that Coppola owes to the opera actually seen in *Godfather III:* that is, to Mascagni's *Cavalleria Rusticana.* Not only does Coppola give a ritualistic cast to violence in ways that call Mascagni to mind, but – as in *Cavalleria Rusticana* – he associates this particular vision of violence with the deeply ceremonial, death-haunted, and religious culture of Sicily.

Set in Sicily, *Cavalleria Rusticana* is based, in fact, on a short story by an Italian author, Giovanni Verga, famous for his tales of Sicilian life. The plot of the opera is fairly simple. It begins on an Easter morning in a small village. A young woman, Santuzza, expresses her dismay that Turridu, the man she loves and to whom she has given her virtue, is nowhere to be seen. She fears that he has returned to an old love, Lola, who is now married to the carter, Alfio. When Turridu returns and treats her roughly, Santuzza's worst fears are confirmed. In a jealous rage, she tells Alfio of his wife's infidelity. The carter hastens off to plot revenge while Santuzza, torn by guilt and fear, runs after him. Now, the organ of a church appears to blend with the orchestra. The service ends; people cluster around the village square while Turridu gaily emerges with Lola and goes off to the tavern to drink happily with his friends. But he is soon confronted by the jealous Alfio and the two men disappear. Before long a scream is heard: an excited village girl reports that Alfio has killed Turridu offstage. And so the curtain falls on a brutal tragedy in a Sicilian village.

The most obvious affinity between *Cavalleria Rusticana* and the *Godfather* films is, I think, the presence of Sicily itself. For in both opera and film, Sicily is not merely a geographical location, an island off the southern coast of Italy; it is, instead, a land ruled by codes of honor, a mythic land where melodramatic dramas of passion and revenge unfold under the sign of destiny. If Mascagni's opera concerns one drama of revenge, Coppola's films insist on the endless family feuds, the deadly vendettas, that have virtually decimated certain Sicilian villages. Significantly, it is here, in this blood-soaked land where feuds and acts of revenge are passed down from one generation to another – a land where, as Michael is told in *Godfather III*, *"sangue chiama sangue"* (i.e., "blood demands blood") – that the saga of the Corleone family begins and ends. A family feud – which will be avenged years later and which presages the many dramas of revenge that punctuate the trilogy – prompts the young Vito to leave Sicily for America where he will establish a dynasty to rival any in his homeland. Years later, Vito's son, Michael, will return to Sicily: there, he will endure the murder of his own daughter and wait for death to take him in his turn.

A melancholy land of origins and endings, Sicily also embodies the destiny that seems to hover over Michael much as it does over the protagonists of *Cavalleria Rusticana*. It is in Sicily that Michael – who has taken refuge in his father's homeland after killing a policeman in New York – appears to make contact with his deepest self, to accept the role that fate has ordained for him. He falls passionately in love with a Sicilian woman and marries her in a simple, old-fashioned ceremony that is in striking contrast to the elaborate festivities that accompany similar occasions in the United States. (Their wedding is marked by the strains of Verdi's most romantic opera, *La Traviata*.) Prompted, in part, by her death, he finally embraces the family role he has rejected for so long. That is, displaying what Joseph Kerman calls the "fierce singleness of operatic passions," he decides to avenge the family honor. When he returns to America, he is a changed man: no longer the casual American we saw at the beginning, he is, instead, a determined, dark-suited son of Sicily.

Deeply linked to Sicilian culture, the dramas of revenge enacted in the *Godfather* films, as in *Cavalleria Rusticana*, have, of course, a naturalistic dimension. The very title of Mascagni's opera hints at this naturalism: "cavalleria rusticana" – which is usually translated as "rustic chivalry," though "rustic honor" might be better – immediately suggests that the opera is concerned not with great historical figures or noble men and women, but, instead, with the lives of humble, ordinary, "rustic" people. Indeed, when Mascangi's work was first performed, its "naturalism" or, to use the

Italian term, *"verismo"* appeared revolutionary in the world of opera. (Garzanti's Italian dictionary defines *verismo* as the "literary movement characterized by the preoccupation with expressing 'truth' and 'nature' even in their crudest forms, that developed in Italy between the end of the 19th century and the beginning of the 20th.") According to the editors of *The Oxford Illustrated History of Opera*, "this one-act opera with its drama of infidelity and revenge among Sicilian peasants launched a vogue for what is known as 'verismo' – the approximate operatic equivalent of literary naturalism" (Parker 198).

Mascagni's opera may well be famous for its *"verismo."* But, at the same time, the naturalistic elements embodied in the opera's humble characters and its "crude" drama of revenge are seen against a backdrop that gives them a deeply ritualistic, ceremonial stamp. As the dialogue constantly reminds us, the action takes place on Easter Sunday. Furthermore, not only are people constantly seen going in and out of the church but music too – the sound of church bells or of an organ – keeps us aware of the church's presence. Most importantly, perhaps, one of the opera's most moving, and famous, musical passages consists of an Easter hymn. Playing a role at once visual, musical, and thematic, these Christian motifs give the drama of revenge, of "rustic chivalry" – one that involves the "rawest" of human emotions – a mythic, even sacred, dimension. Observing that the "secret" of Mascagni's opera lay, precisely, in the "interplay of rite and personal action," W. H. Auden declared that the personal tragedy of the characters "is seen against an immense background, the recurrent death and rebirth of nature, the liturgical celebration of the once-and-for-all death and resurrection of the redeemer of man . . . so that their local history takes on a ritual significance" (Auden, 480).

The "ritual significance" that Auden perceives in *Cavalleria Rusticana* takes us to the heart, I would argue, of Coppola's esthetic in the *Godfather* trilogy. Here, what might be seen as the tradition of American naturalism – embodied, say, in the realistic details of American life or in the acting and dialogue – is transformed by a ritualistic context largely created by the presence of images and rites associated with Christianity. Moreover, this context is most in evidence when the film depicts key scenes of violence: that is, in those scenes depicting the ascension of each new Don. Providing an "immense backdrop" for what are essentially local struggles, this Christian context transforms sequences that, if depicted in a totally naturalistic manner, would be little more the "crudest" of power struggles or bloodbaths. This is not to say that the *Godfather* films display the same, fairly specific, "liturgical celebration" that Auden perceives in *Cavalleria Rusticana*. But the "immense backdrop" created by Christian iconography and ritual does create the sense that we are witnessing a titanic struggle between good and evil rather than a mere battle or skirmish between rival gangs or Mafia families. This is a battle in which, as we move from past to present, the forces of evil grow stronger and stronger even as they pull us into an escalating cycle of apocalyptic violence and spreading moral decay.

Thus, the murder that Vito (Robert de Niro) must commit to gain power in *Godfather II* has an innocent, celebratory cast that will vanish when it comes time for his son to take his place. If murder can ever be justified, the one Vito commits would surely fall into that category: his victim, Don Fanucci, is a greedy and cruel boss who tyrannizes the neighborhood and who has cost Vito his job. But if this scene is imbued with an innocence soon to be lost, the *manner* in which Coppola depicts Vito's triumph will be echoed – and amplified – in similar sequences concerning Michael and, later, Vincenzo. That is, here – as he will do later – Coppola underscores what Auden calls the interplay of "rite and personal action" in *Cavalleria Rusticana*. Almost as if he were paying homage to Mascagni – as, indeed, he will do in his next film – in this critical sequence Coppola juxtaposes scenes of Vito stalking his prey from the rooftops of New York with those of a religious procession passing through the streets of Little Italy. Seen dramatically from overhead, the procession might well be a kind of theatrical performance. Processional music is heard as the critical moment of primal violence – which will launch the Corleone family on the road to money and power – comes ever nearer. The procession comes to a halt; Don Fanucci, dressed in a gleaming white suit, mounts the steps to his apartment – only to see Vito waiting for him in the darkness. The latter shoots; bloodstains spread over the old man's white suit; festive music from outside suddenly begins anew as firecrackers are launched. When a triumphant Vito merges with the street crowd, its cheers and festivities now appear to celebrate the deadly ritual he has just completed. As he rejoins his family and caresses his new baby, the strains of an old Italian lullaby are heard. All is well, this song suggests, the initiation to violence, the ceremony, is over.

The festive overtones of this scene vanish, as I have suggested, when it is Michael's turn to consolidate power and win respect as the new Don. The innocence that marked Vito's action – and, to some extent, his life – has disappeared into the folds of the past. But even as sin and transgression come to the fore, so too does the ceremonial cast of the scene become more insistent. To begin with, we are no longer watching a religious procession pass by; rather, we are in the church. There, an important rite is being performed: Connie's young son – for whom Michael has agreed to act as godfather – is about to be baptized. Once again, the rhythm and tension mount as scenes of holy rituals are juxtaposed with those of violence. As the service begins, the killers engaged by Michael carefully prepare their weapons: they are about to assassinate the important members of the five crime families that threaten the Corleones. When the killing finally starts, the words of the rite grow louder and more frenzied while the sacred music swells ominously. The immeasurable gap between the sacred rituals of the church and the unholy rites of the killers – in the end, the gap between good and evil – is underscored still further by Michael's conduct within the church. When asked a series of ritual questions by the priest, the man who has masterminded all the killings does not flinch as he answers: "Yes, I have renounced Satan and all his works. Yes, I am ready to be baptized." Like the killings, these sacreligeous lies tell us how far he has fallen from grace, how binding is the pact he has made with the devil.

The clash between good and evil seen in this sequence becomes more epic still in *Godfather III*. Not only has the Vatican itself (or corrupt Vatican officials) been drawn into the struggle, but – giving a demonic cast to the scene – one of the worst assassins has disguised himself as a priest. (This recalls a similar disguise used by an assassin during the baptismal rite. The earlier killer, however, was disguised not as a "false priest" but as a policeman.) This time, moreover, the implicit homage to *Cavalleria Rusticana* seen earlier has become explicit. Turning Mascagni's opera and his film into reflecting mirrors of one another, Coppola stages this last epic struggle during a performance of *Cavalleria Rusticana*. Thus, the church that figured in the baptismal rite has given way to the Palermo opera house; the Christian ceremonies that are intercut with brutal scenes of violence are those performed on stage. Significantly, though, Coppola adds to the dramatic intensity of these staged rites: he moves Mascagni's hymn sequence toward the end of the opera – so that the liturgical music peaks at the same time as the violence – even as he places striking figures of hooded penitents and effigies of death into the staged religious procession. Underscoring the colossal nature of the battle between good and evil, these dramatic additions and changes also allow him to comment explicitly on some of the bloody actions taking place offstage. Indeed, one particularly effective cut suggests that the apparent heart attack of a newly elected Pope was really a murder designed to prevent him from investigating some of the Vatican's shady financial dealings. This cut takes us from the staged figure of Christ upon the cross to a chamber in the Vatican where a woman screams upon discovering the dead body of the Pope.

In *Godfather III*, then, the ritualistic clash between good and evil leads – as never before – into the very heart of Christendom. This time, too, the clash does not come to an end when the rite is complete. Quite the contrary: after the performance ends, the epic battles of melodrama give way to the starkness of tragedy. As Mary dies upon the steps of the opera house, violence assumes – arguably, for the first time in the trilogy – the sacred dimension that Auden perceived in *Cavalleria Rusticana*. Thus, it is all the more telling that, as she dies, Mascagni's music begins to swell once again. As the music recalls the opera to us, a scream from Mary's mother, Kay, seems to echo the scream uttered onstage when Turridu, played by the Corleone son, was murdered at the end of *Cavalleria Rusticana*. To Kay's child who died on stage must now be added this second child whose death, alas, is all too real. Michael, too, is seen screaming. But, for a few seemingly endless seconds, his scream is soundless – seen but not heard. The place of the scream we do not hear is filled, instead, by Mascagni's music – as if it alone could express the depth of Michael's anguish and grief. Nor does Mascagni's music come to a halt at this point. Now imbued with the tragedy of the Corleone family, it accompanies three flashback scenes depicting moments of past joy that intensify the horror of the present. Michael is seen dancing with the women he loved and lost: his daughter, his Sicilian bride, his ex-wife, Kay. Only when the film closes with Michael's death does the opera – by now one with the film – come to an end.

The finale of *Godfather III* clearly sets the tragedy of the Corleone family under the sign of *Cavalleria Rusticana*. But the manner and meaning of Mary's death resonate, inevitably, with the strains of still another opera. For if Mascagni points to cast of the film, a cast deeply embedded in Sicilian culture, this second opera echoes, instead, the personal tragedy that befalls Michael and his family. I am speaking now of one of the most famous works in the operatic repertory: that is, of Verdi's *Rigoletto* (1851). Usually seen as the beginning of Verdi's first period of brilliance, *Rigoletto* depicts the drama embodied in the culminating sequences of *Godfather III*. That is, like Coppola's film, Verdi's opera portrays the tragic death of a beautiful and cherished daughter who perishes because of the sins of her father.

Although *Rigoletto* is never mentioned explicitly, one of the many performances that punctuate the trilogy – in this case, a Punch-and-Judy show witnessed by Michael and Kay in the course of an afternoon excursion in Sicily – hints at the father/daughter drama informing both *Rigoletto* and *Godfather III*. Before an enraptured audience in the village square, the puppets act out the drama of a young princess who feels a forbidden love for her cousin – a love that inevitably evokes that between Mary and Vincenzo. But whereas Michael simply tells Vincenzo that such a marriage would be impossible, the princess's father reacts in true melodramatic fashion. That is, to save his daughter from this guilty love, the king stabs her through the heart to the gasps of the wide-eyed spectators.

Rigoletto, of course, does not perform such a heinous deed himself. But there is never any doubt that he – like Michael in *Godfather III* – is responsible for his daughter's death. In Verdi's opera, which is based upon a play by Victor Hugo, *Le roi s'amuse* (1832), Rigoletto is a mean-spirited, hunchbacked jester at the court of a corrupt Renaissance prince, the Duke of Mantua. The self-hatred inspired in him by his deformity also incites him to treat others with cruelty and viciousness. Thus, he goads the libertine duke to seduce any woman who appeals to him even if she is the wife or daughter of one of the duke's courtiers. Describing the evil hunchback, Victor Hugo noted that the only pastime of his protagonist "is making endless trouble between the nobles and their king, playing the strong against the weak. He absolutely depraves the king, enticing him to every kind of viciousness. He introduces him to respectable families, all the while pointing out which wife to seduce, which sister to entice, which daughter to debauch. In [his] hands the king is just a puppet" (Godefroy, 189). It is, in fact, this "taste for trouble" and depravity that bring down an ominous curse upon Rigoletto. For when the desperate father of one of the duke's many victims gives vent to his anger and grief, Rigoletto arrogantly mocks him, saying, "Why this nonsense about your daughter's honor?" This cruel barb prompts the unhappy man to utter a "solemn malediction" upon the duke and Rigoletto. (The original title of the opera was, in fact, *La Maledizione*, that is, "The Curse.")

While the duke shrugs off this ominous curse, Rigoletto, instead, begins to brood. He is worried, above all, that a disaster will befall the only being he loves: his beautiful daughter, Gilda. And, indeed, the curse does begin to make itself felt. Despite Rigoletto's many precautions, the duke (disguised as a poor student) sees Gilda in church and begins to woo her. But worse is to come: the courtiers, who hate Rigoletto for his cruel tongue and vicious jokes, decide to play a trick on the hunchback. In the belief that Gilda is Rigoletto's mistress rather than his daughter, they trick Rigoletto into helping them abduct her to the palace. When Rigoletto realizes what has happened, he rushes to the palace. But he is too late: the duke has already taken his daughter's honor. Now Rigoletto is as outraged and desperate as the fathers and husbands he so cruelly mocked. In despair, he hires an assassin to kill the duke and arranges to have the latter's body brought to him in a sack. But the plot misfires. Gilda, who loves the duke and is heartbroken when she learns of his philandering, decides to sacrifice herself for her lover. When Rigotletto opens the sack supposedly containing the duke's body, he finds, instead, that of his dying daughter. She lingers only long enough to bid her father adieu, telling him that she will join her mother in heaven and pray for him. As she expires in her father's arms, he collapses over her lifeless body.

As in the case of *Cavalleria Rusticana,* the analogies between *Rigoletto* and the *Godfather* trilogy (particularly *Godfather III*) extend beyond a single parallel: in this case, the terrible fate met by a father and daughter. For the dominant motifs of the *Godfather* films – which bear upon family and power – are rooted in the same melodramatic substratum so clearly visible in *Rigoletto.* Indeed, according to Catherine Clement, such motifs are the core of virtually all opera. In a book whose very title assumes a certain resonance in light of Mary's death – that is, *Opera, or the Undoing of Women* – Clement argues that opera is always about transgressions committed against patriarchy, authority, power. Operatic characters die, she writes, "for transgression – for transgression of familial rules, political rules, the things at stake in sexual and authoritarian power" (Clement, 10).

In the case of Verdi's operas, in particular, as Clement reminds us, not only were issues related to power especially marked but, frequently, they were endowed with an ideological or political cast. A great Italian nationalist, Verdi was deeply influenced by the revolutionary stirrings surrounding the Risorgimento, the movement for Italian liberation.[1] "In the age following the triumvirate of Rossini, Bellini and Donizetti," write the editors of *The Metropolitan Opera Guide*, "a new spirit permeated all phases of life in Italy. The rumblings of national revolt and liberation from the Austrian yoke made themselves felt in the music of the day. . . . Italian opera throbbed with a hot-blood vitality" (Peltz and Lawrence, 193). This revolutionary spirit is voiced most explicitly, of course, in Verdi's great epic operas – that is, in works such as *Nabucco, I Lombardi, Don Carlo,* and *Aida* which deal with the destinies of peoples, of nations. The yearning for liberty and national autonomy that swept over Europe in the middle of the previous century is heard in the chorus of the Hebrew slaves in *Nabucco,* in the stirring toast to "Liberta" in *Don Carlo,* and in melancholy strains of the exiled, enslaved heroine of *Aida.* But, as Clement suggests, even an intimate work such as *La Traviata* – a drama in which a courtesan sacrifices herself for the sake of the family of the man she loves – deals with "power" and "transgression." *La Traviata,* writes Clement, "is the exemplary history of a woman crushed by the bourgeois family, exemplary because the entire history of opera pivots around things at stake in the family. There is the common law, there are fathers to defend and apply it, and there are rebels" (Clement, 60).

I would not follow Clement in placing every opera under the sign of transgression and power. But, certainly, these *were* powerful impulses in Verdi. And, even more than in *La Traviata,* the family drama enacted in *Rigoletto* involves such impulses. After all, the two male protagonists of this work possess all the authority usually invested in a father, a ruler. And it is for *their* transgressions that Gilda dies and Rigoletto is punished. No less than the famous libertine of Mozart's *Don Giovanni,* Rigoletto scoffs at the bonds of love and family, at the codes demanded by virtue and honor. And the arrogant and callous duke, who abuses his power with men and women, is almost as blameworthy as his twisted jester. Indeed, Hugo's portrait of an aristocratic villain was so unflattering that Verdi was forced to alter the original play in significant ways. That is, in *Le roi s'amuse,* the noble villain was a French king rather than an Italian duke: hence, the title *Le roi s'amuse (The king enjoys himself)*. (Hugo's harsh portrait of a French king was probably the reason the play was banned in France, although the reason given was its "depravity.") To enable the opera to be produced in Italy, Verdi had to come to an agreement with the censor representing the Austrian authorities who ruled much of Italy at the time. Fearful of the revolutionary and nationalist spirit that was sweeping over Europe, the authorities, as Ernest Newman notes, did not consider it "advisable that a king . . . should be shown to the Italian people in so unfavorable a light" (Newman, 45). Thus, Verdi changed the figure of the king to that of a provincial duke and gave the opera a new title: hence, *Rigoletto*.

Whether duke or king, however, Verdi's powerful ruler lives in the same climate of moral corruption and cynicism, of intrigue and conspiracy, as that which bathes the Corleone fortress in Lake Tahoe. But the most important analogy between Coppola's film and Verdi's opera in terms of power and transgression bears, of course, upon the way Michael Corleone destroys the family and abuses the authority invested in him as head of the Corleones. As suggested earlier, his descent into a maelstrom of evil is first made clear in the baptismal sequence when he lies in church and takes communion with an unclean soul. From that point on, one sin follows another: he kills his sister's husband, separates his wife from their children after they divorce. Embracing power and murder for their own sake, he ignores a cardinal rule of "business" by having men killed when nothing is to be gained. Worst of all, he has his older brother Fredo put to death as the latter is reciting a "Hail Mary" in a small fishing boat. "On shore," writes William McDonald of this scene, "gazing out from a window at the family compound, stands the stony figure of Michael Corleone, his transformation to monster now complete, having lost his soul as surely as Fredo's had departed" (McDonald, 11).

Whereas *Godfather II* traces Michael's "transformation to monster," *Godfather III* presents, instead, a man deeply troubled by past sins. Haunted by remorse for his deeds, in this film Michael – who has never confided in anyone – finally confesses his sins to a priest. In one of the most moving sequences of the film, he breaks down and cries, "I have killed my mother's son." But repentence has come too late. For his sins, for his inability to change his life, Michael – like Rigoletto – will see the being he most loves taken from him. And – to further atone for his arrogance and crimes – he will be condemned to live with the terrible burden of knowing that the guilt was his. With Mary's death, as with Gilda's in *Rigoletto*, the "curse" is fulfilled; the ritual of crime and punishment has come to an end.

If Michael's tragedy recalls that of Rigoletto, the *Godfather* trilogy as a whole is imbued with the shadow of Verdi in still another way. Less palpable than the operatic analogies with *Cavalleria Rusticana* and *Rigoletto* suggested thus far, this resemblance does not involve specific characters or situations. Rather, it bears upon the way the films both spring from, and reflect, a larger historical and social context. As suggested earlier, Verdi's operas – in particular, his epic works like *Aida* and *Don Carlo* – were particularly deeply rooted in the climate of his time, in the revolutionary and nationalistic currents surrounding the Risorgimento. I would suggest that, in a similar way, the *Godfather* films also open upon the broader stage of national history. For, as many commentators have sensed, behind the tragic tale of the Corleones lies the specter of modern American history. And it is here – that is, in the ways in which the *Godfather* films filter history through a family saga – that their operatic dimension takes on the particular cast seen in the films by the two Italian directors mentioned at the beginning of this study: that is, Visconti and Bertolucci.

Like the *Godfather* trilogy, films such as Visconti's *The Leopard* (*Il Gattopardo*, 1963) and *The Damned* (*La Caduta degli Dei*, 1969) as well as Bertolucci's *1900* (*Novecento*, 1976) and *The Last Emperor* (1987) use all the operatic strategies discussed thus far – that is, choral moments, visual and aural leitmotifs, a heightened ceremonial and melodramatic cast – to intensify the epic, national sweep of family sagas. In what may be the greatest work of this kind (that is, *The Leopard*), Visconti traces the decline of the Italian aristocracy and the rise of bourgeosie in the nineteenth century through the characters of the noble Prince of Salina and his nephew Tancredi. In a similar manner, in *1900*, a six-hour epic that begins, significantly, with the death of Verdi in 1901, Bertolucci uses two families, with interlocking destinies, to portray the rise of Italian fascism.

Like *The Leopard* and *1900*, the Godfather films leave no doubt that the epic, operatic saga of the Corleones embodies (represents) that of the nation. It has not gone unnoticed that the opening words of *The Godfather*, spoken by a petitioner to Don Vito whose daughter has been beaten and abused by two young men, are: "I believe in America." But even as he speaks these words, it is clear – since the two young men have barely been punished – that his belief is unjustified, that justice has not been served. By the end of *Godfather II*, this opening comment finds a dark echo in a somber observation made by Michael: "If history has taught us anything," he says, "it is that you can kill anybody." Framing the films, these remarks point to the immense moral distance traveled by the Corleones even as they suggest the national dimension of this family saga. That is, behind the drama of a Sicilian-American Don who betrays what he most reveres – the family – lies the agony of an America that has lost its moral compass.

The deliberately epic and national aspects of the trilogy are probably most in evidence in *Godfather II*. Taking us further back into the past than *The Godfather* itself – that is, to Vito's arrival in America – it encompasses a larger span of time, and of history, than either *The Godfather* or *Godfather III*. This allows it to trace, through the rising fortunes of the Corleone family, critical shifts and changes in American life: the dissolution of the family, the assimilation of immigrants, the move from city to suburb, a shift from east to west. But the most important of these changes is undoubtedly a moral one: for even as the Corleone family moves into the mainstream of American life, so, too, do its ruthless and violent tactics. Whether or not, as commentators such as John Hess have suggested, the rise of the Corleone Mafia family can be seen as a parable about the ruthless course of capitalist America (Hess, 81–90), dialogue and actions repeatedly confirm that the

"American way of life," based on business, is no different from the criminal "business" of the Corleone family. When Michael takes his place next to powerful CEOs and government officials during an important meeting in Cuba, we know, of course, that the Corleones have arrived. At the same time, and just as surely, we also know that all endorse and share their criminal tactics. The most dramatic, and telling, of these changes, of course, is the transformation of Michael Corleone himself. His terrifying evolution – from World War II hero to power-crazed, paranoid murderer who sees enemies everywhere – mirrors a path that, in the wake of Vietnam, many felt America itself had traveled. The lone figure of Michael who has just killed his brother and who stands shrouded in darkness at the end of *Godfather II* suggests the powerful yet impotent imperial power defeated for the first time in its history.

But if the film is a lament for what America has become, it is also a celebration of what America was. The flashbacks of Vito's arrival in America, and of immigrant life in Little Italy in the early years of the century, do more than add to the film's epic dimension. Consistently underscored by all the operatic strategies discussed earlier, they also give rise to the overwhelming nostalgia that pervades the film. The golden-hued tones of immigrant life in Little Italy, where warmth fills the cramped apartments and people jostle one another in the teeming streets, glow even brighter in contrast with the snowclad landscape, drained of color and life, of the bleak family estate in Nevada. Recalling the warmth of the Corleone family life, these shots clearly recall a welcoming America, a land of dream and myth. Shot in soft focus and sepia tones, flashbacks of tenement streets or Ellis Island evoke iconic photographs of early twentieth-century New York life: reviewers Leonard Quart and Albert Auster suggest in fact that such scenes resemble famous photographs by Jacob Riis and Lewis Hines (Quart and Auster, 39). Like those photographs, these scenes, too, exude both the sense of death and the aching nostalgia for the past that always cling to photography. "Photography," comments Susan Sontag, "is an elegiac art, a twilight art . . . All photographs are momenti mori" (Sontag, 15); whether or not the subject of a photograph is dead, declares Roland Barthes, the photograph itself speaks of "this catastrophe" (Barthes, 96).

Imbued with mourning for a lost America, the *Godfather* films – and here, for once, Coppola's films are in sharp contrast with Verdi's operas – speak not of a nation about to be born but of one in decline. The image of America they evoke is one of an imperial power forced to confront its crimes from the downward slope of history. But the very image of such a power suggests one last analogy with opera. Admittedly the most speculative of the analogies adressed thus far, it is prompted by an observation made by Catherine Clement. In her view, one has only to glance at some of the most famous of operatic works to see in them

> the history of our various imperialisms: *Tosca,* or Bonaparte invading Italy in the name of the ideals of the French Revolution; *Butterfly,* or Meiji Japan subjugated by the whiskey of an American naval officer; *Carmen,* or the yet unfinished Gypsy rebellion, still in the course of history; *Othello,* or the Moor who is a traitor to his color in the name of the Republic of Venice; *Tristan and Isolde,* or Ireland carried off by Britain. . . . Like a vast unwinding written in passions and daggers, the whole history of a West bound to represent lyrically its own crime – prey to its own mastery, weeping over its massacres – calmly emerges from this limited spectacle reduced to love stories. (Clement, 107)

By no stretch of the imagination might the *Godfather* films be considered love stories. Still, in another sense, they too might be seen as inheritors of this operatic tradition: that is, of a tradition in which the West – after exerting its imperial might and commiting its crimes – sees, enjoys those crimes turned into spectacle. In this case, it is the melancholy yet mesmerizing spectacle of the rise and fall of a Mafia family.

NOTE

1. Verdi's deep connection to the "spirit" of his times was certainly one of the factors that prompted the great Italian Marxist, Antonio Gramsci, to posit a relationship between the flowering of nineteenth-century Italian opera and the revolutionary impulse of the

Risorgimento. It was Gramsci's view that, in Italy, opera played the kind of "national-popular" role that, in other countries, fell to popular novelists. That is, not only was it nourished in a particular political climate and in the soil of popular culture, but its very popularity suggested that it came from, and spoke to, the people. Gramsci's remarks on Verdi and opera are scattered throughout his *Letterature e vita nazionale* (Rome: Riuniti, 1977).

BIBLIOGRAPHY

Auden, W. H. *The Dyer's Hand*. New York: Random House, 1962.

Barthes, Roland. *La camera chiara*. Rome: Einaudi, 1980.

Clement, Catherine. *Opera, or the Undoing of Women*, trans. Betsy Wing. Minneapolis: University of Minnesota Press, 1988.

Vincent Godefroy. *The Dramatic Genius of Verdi: Studies of Selected Operas*, Vol. 1. New York: St. Martin's Press, 1975.

Hess, John. *"Godfather II:* A Deal Coppola Couldn't Refuse," in *Movies and Methods*, ed. Bill Nichols. Berkeley: University of California Press, 1976, 81–90.

Kerman, Joseph. *Opera as Drama*. Berkeley: University of California Press, 1988. Originally published by Knopf in 1956.

McDonald, William. "Thicker Than Water, and Spilled by the Mob." *The New York Times* 21 (May 1995), Sec. H: 11, 20.

Newman, Ernest. *Stories of the Great Operas*. New York: Knopf, 1930.

Parker, Roger, ed. *The Oxford Illustrated History of Opera*. Oxford and New York: Oxford University Press, 1994.

Peltz, Mary Ellis, and Robert Lawrence. *The Metropolitan Opera Guide*. New York: Random House, 1947.

Poizat, Michel. *The Angel's Cry: Beyond the Pleasure Principle in Opera*, trans. Arthur Denner. Ithaca, NY and London: Cornell University Press, 1992.

Quart, Leonard, and Albert Auster. *"The Godfather: Part II,"* Cineaste 6(4) (1974), 38–39.

Sontag, Susan. *On Photography*. New York: Delta, 1977.

Filmography

1963

Dementia 13

Script: Francis Ford Coppola
Director: Francis Ford Coppola
Editing: Stuart O'Brien
Photography: Charles Hannawalt
Art Director: Albert Locatelli
Producer: Roger Corman
Production Company: American International Pictures Productions
Cast: William Campbell, Luana Anders, Bart Patton, Mary
  Mitchell, Patrick Magee, Ethne Dunne, Peter Read, Karl
  Schanzer, Ron Perry, Derry O'Donovan, Barbara Dowling

1967

You're a Big Boy Now

Script: Francis Ford Coppola, from the novel of David Benedictus
Director: Francis Ford Coppola
Editing: Aram Avakian
Photography: Andrew Laszlo
Music: Bob Prince
Art Director: Vassele Fotopoulos
Costumes: Theoni V. Aldredge

Choreography: Robert Tucker

Producer: Phil Feldman

Production Company: Seven Arts

Cast: Peter Kastner, Elizabeth Hartman, Geraldine Page, Julie Harris, Rip Torn, Michael Dunn, Tony Bill, Karen Black, Dolph Sweet, Michael O'Sullivan

1968

Finian's Rainbow

Script: E. Y. Harburg and Fred Saidy

Director: Francis Ford Coppola

Editing: Melvin Shapiro

Photography: Philip Lathrop

Sound: M. A. Merrick, Dan Wallin

Music: Burton Lane

Production Designer: Hilyard M. Brown

Costumes: Dorothy Jeakins

Choreography: Hermes Pan

Producer: Joseph Landon

Production Company: Warner Brothers–Seven Arts

Cast: Fred Astaire, Petula Clark, Tommy Steele, Don Francks, Keenan Wynn, Al Freeman Jr., Barbara Hancock, Ronald Colby, Dolph Sweet, Wright King, Louis Silas, Brenda Arnau

1969

The Rain People

Script: Francis Ford Coppola

Director: Francis Ford Coppola

Editing: Blackie Malkin

Photography: Wilmer Butler

Sound: Nathan Boxer

Music: Ronald Stein

Art Director: Leon Ericksen

Producer: Bart Patton and Ronald Colby

Production Company: American Zoetrope

Cast: Shirley Knight, James Caan, Robert Duvall, Marya Zimmet, Tom Aldredge, Laurie Crewes, Andrew Duncan, Margaret Fairchild, Sally Gracie, Alan Manson, Robert Modica

1972

The Godfather

Script: Mario Puzo and Francis Ford Coppola, based on the novel by Puzo

Director: Francis Ford Coppola

Editing: William Reynolds and Peter Zinner

Photography: Gordon Willis

Sound: Christopher Newman

Music: Nino Rota

Production Designer: Dean Tavoularis

Art Director: Warren Clymer

Costumes: Anna Hill Johnstone

Producer: Albert S. Ruddy

Production Company: Alfran Productions, Inc.

Cast: Marlon Brando, Al Pacino, James Caan, Richard Castellano, Robert Duvall, Sterling Hayden, John Marley, Richard Conte, Al Lettieri, Diane Keaton, Abe Vigoda, Talia Shire, Gianni Russo, John Cazale, Rudy Bond, Al Martino, Morgana King, Lenny Montana, John Martino, Salvatore Corsitto, Richard Bright, Alex Rocco, Tony Giorgio

1974

The Conversation

Script: Francis Ford Coppola

Director: Francis Ford Coppola

Editing: Richard Chew

Photography: Bill Butler

Sound: Walter Murch

Music: David Shire

Production Designer: Dean Tavoularis

Costumes: Aggie Guerard Rodgers

Producer: Fred Roos

Production Company: The Director's Company Presents a Coppola Company Production

Cast: Gene Hackman, John Cazale, Allen Garfield, Frederick Forrest, Cindy Williams, Michael Higgins, Elizabeth MacRae, Terri Garr, Harrison Ford, Robert Duvall, Mark Wheeler, Robert Shields, Phoebe Alexander

The Godfather Part II

Script: Francis Ford Coppola and Mario Puzo, based on the novel by Puzo

Director: Francis Ford Coppola

Editing: Peter Zinner, Barry Malkin, Richard Marks

Photography: Gordon Willis

Sound: Walter Murch

Music: Nino Rota

Production Designer: Dean Tavoularis

Art Director: Angelo Graham

Costumes: Theadora Van Runkle

Producer: Francis Ford Coppola

Production Company: The Coppola Company

Cast: Al Pacino, Robert Duvall, Diane Keaton, Robert De Niro, John Cazale, Talia Shire, Lee Strasberg, Michael V. Gazzo, G. D. Spradlin, Richard Bright, Gaston Moschin, Tom Rosqui, B. Kirby Jr., Frank Sivero, Francesca DeSapio, Morgana King, Mariana Hill, Leopoldo Trieste, Dominic Chianese, Amerigo Tot, Troy Donahue, John Aprea, Joe Spinell

1979

Apocalypse Now

Script: John Milius and Francis Coppola

Director: Francis Ford Coppola

Editing: Walter Murch, Gerald B. Greenberg, Lisa Fruchtman, and Richard Marks

Photography: Vittorio Storaro

Sound: Walter Murch

Music: Carmine Coppola and Francis Ford Coppola

Production Designer: Dean Tavoularis

Art Director: Angelo Graham

Costumes: Charles E. James

Producer: Francis Ford Coppola

Production Company: Omni Zoetrope

Cast: Marlon Brando, Robert Duvall, Martin Sheen, Frederick Forrest, Albert Hall, Sam Bottoms, Larry Fishburne, Dennis Hopper, G. D. Spradlin, Harrison Ford, Jerry Ziesmer, Scott Glen

1982

One from the Heart

Script: Armyan Bernstein and Francis Ford Coppola

Director: Francis Ford Coppola

Editing: Anne Goursaud, with Rudi Fehr and Randy Roberts

Photography: Vittorio Storaro

Sound: Richard Beggs

Music: Tom Waits

Production Designer: Dean Tavoularis

Art Director: Angelo Graham

Costumes: Ruth Morley

Choreography: Kenny Ortega

Producer: Gray Fredrickson and Fred Roos

Production Company: Zoetrope Studios

Cast: Frederick Forrest, Terri Garr, Raul Julia, Nastassia Kinski, Lainie Kasan, Harry Dean Stanton, Allen Goorwitz, Jeff Hamlin, Italia Coppola, Carmine Coppola

1983

The Outsiders

Script: Kathleen Knutsen Rowell, from the novel by S. E. Hinton

Director: Francis Ford Coppola

Editing: Anne Goursaud

Photography: Stephen H. Burum

Sound: Richard Beggs

Music: Carmine Coppola

Production Designer: Dean Tavoularis

Costumes: Marge Bowers

Producer: Fred Roos and Gray Fredrickson

Production Company: Zoetrope Studios

Cast: Matt Dillon, Ralph Macchio, C. Thomas Howell, Patrick Swayze, Rob Lowe, Emilio Estevez, Tom Cruise, Glenn Withrow, Diane Lane, Leif Garret, Darren Dalton, Michelle Meyrink, Gailard Sartain, Tom Waits, William Smith

Rumble Fish

Script: S. E. Hilton and Francis Ford Coppola

Director: Francis Ford Coppola

Editing: Barry Malkin

Photography: Stephen H. Burum

Sound: Richard Beggs

Music: Stewart Copeland

Production Design: Dean Tavoularis

Costumes: Marge Bowers

Producer: Fred Roos and Doug Clayboure

Production Company: Zoetrope Studios

Cast: Matt Dillon, Mickey Rourke, Diane Lane, Dennis Hopper, Diana Scarwid, Vincent Spano, Nicholas Cage, Christopher Penn, Larry Fishburne, William Smith, Michael Higgins, Glenn Withrow, Tom Waits, Herb Rice, Maybelle Wallace, Nona Manning, Domino, Gio, S. E. Hinton

1984

The Cotton Club

Script: William Kennedy and Francis Ford Coppola

Director: Francis Ford Coppola

Editing: Barry Malkin and Robert Q. Lovett

Photography: Stephen Goldblatt

Sound: Edward Beyer

Music: John Barry and Bob Wilber

Production Designer: Richard Sylbert

Costumes: Milena Canonero

Choreography: Michael Smuin

Producer: Robert Evans

Cast: Richard Gere, Gregory Hines, Diane Lane, Lonette McKee, Bob Hoskins, James Remar, Nicholas Cage, Allen Garfield, Fred Gwynne, Gwen Verdon, Lisa Jane Persky, Maurice Hines, Julian Beck, Novella Nelson, Larry Fishbourne, John Ryan, Tom Waits

1986

Peggy Sue Got Married

Script: Jerry Leichting and Arlene Sarner

Director: Francis Ford Coppola

Editing: Barry Malkin

Photography: Jordan Cronenweth

Sound: Michael Kirchberger

Music: John Barry

Production Designer: Dean Tavoularis

Art Director: Alex Tavoularis

Costumes: Theadora Van Runkle

Producer: Paul R. Gurian

Production Company: Zoetrope Studios Production

Cast: Kathleen Turner, Nicolas Cage, Barry Miller, Catherine Hicks, Joan Allen, Kevin J. O'Connor, Jim Carrey, Lisa Jane

Persky, Lucinda Jenney, Will Shriner, Barbara Harris, Don Murray, Sofia Coppola, Maureen O'Sullivan, Leon Ames

1987

Garden of Stone

Script: Ronald Bass, based on the novel by Nicholas Proffit

Director: Francis Ford Coppola

Editing: Barry Malkin

Photography: Jordan Cronenweth

Sound: Richard Beggs

Music: Carmine Coppola

Production Designer: Dean Tavoularis

Art Director: Alex Tavoularis

Costumes: Willa Kim and Judianna Makovsky

Producer: Michael I. Levy and Francis Ford Coppola

Production Company: Tri-Star-ML Delphi Premier Production

Cast: James Caan, Anjelica Houston, James Earl Jones, D. B. Sweeney, Dean Stockwell, Mary Stuart Masterson, Dick Anthony Williams, Lonette McKee, Sam Bottoms, Elias Koteas, Larry Fishburne, Casey Siemaszko, Peter Masterson, Carlin Glynn, Erick Holland, Bill Graham

1988

Tucker, The Man and His Dream

Script: Arnold Schulman and David Seidler

Director: Francis Ford Coppola

Editing: Priscilla Ned

Photography: Vittorio Storaro

Sound: Richard Beggs

Music: Joe Jackson

Production Designer: Dean Tavoularis

Art Director: Alex Tavoularis

Costumes: Milena Canonero

Producer: Fred Roos and Fred Fuchs

Production Company: Lucasfilm Ltd.

Cast: Jeff Bridges, Joan Allen, Martin Landau, Frederick Forrest, Elias Koteas, Christian Slater, Nina Siemaszko, Anders Johnson, Corky Nemec, Marshall Bell, Jay O. Saunders, Peter Donat, Dean Goodman, John X. Heart, Don Novello, Patti Austin, Sandy Bull, Joseph Miksak, Scott Beach, Roland Scrivner, Howard Hughes, Bob Safford, Larry Menkin, Ron Close, Joe Flood

1990

The Godfather Part III

Script: Mario Puzo and Francis Ford Coppola

Director: Francis Ford Coppola

Editing: Barry Malkin

Photography: Gordon Willis

Music: Carmine Coppola

Production Designer: Dean Tavoularis

Art Director: Alex Tavoularis

Costumes: Milena Canonero

Producer: Francis Ford Coppola

Production Company: Zoetrope Studios/Paramount

Cast: Al Pacino, Talia Shire, Diane Keaton, Andy Garcia, Franc D'Ambrosio, Sofia Coppola, John Savage, Eli Wallach, Donal Donnelly, Richard Bright, Al Martino, Joe Mantegna, George Hamilton, Robert Cicchini, Terri Liverano Baker, Bridget Fonda, Raf Vallone, Mario Donatone, Vittorio Duse

1992

Bram Stoker's Dracula

Script: James V. Hart

Director: Francis Ford Coppola

Editing: Nicholas C. Smith

Photography: Michael Ballhaus

Sound: Leslie Schatz

Music: Wojciech Kilar

Production Designer: Thomas Sanders

Art Director: Andrew Precht

Costumes: Eiko Ishioka

Producer: Francis Ford Coppola, Fred Fuchs, and Charles Mulvehill

Production Company: American Zoetrope/Osiris Films

Cast: Gary Oldman, Winona Ryder, Anthony Hopkins, Keanu
    Reeves, Richard E. Grant, Cary Elwes, Bill Campbell, Sadie Frost,
    Tom Waits

Reviews of
The Godfather Trilogy

KEEPING UP WITH THE CORLEONES

WILLIAM PECHTER

Reprinted from *Commentary,* vol. 54, no. 1, July 1972, by permission; all rights reserved.

In one of my earliest appearances in *Commentary* ("With-It Movies," February 1970) I wrote in praise of Francis Ford Coppola's *The Rain People,* a film I had little company in finding favor with. Coppola is a young director whose career occupies a curious middle ground between a Peter Bogdanovich's accommodation to the Hollywood Establishment and a Dennis Hopper's rebellion against it. Before *The Rain People,* his first uncompromisingly "personal" film, Coppola had directed three films of which two were low-budget "little" films and the other a big musical. After the critical and commercial failure of *The Rain People,* Coppola went on to win an Academy Award for co-authoring the screenplay of *Patton* (a film he didn't direct), and has now directed *The Godfather,* a film which is not only Coppola's first big popular success as a director but seems further destined to be among the two or three most commercially successful movies of all time.

And *The Godfather* is, furthermore, and by critical consensus, a stunning confirmation of my claims for Coppola's talents: vividly seen, richly detailed, throbbing with incident and a profusion of strikingly drawn characters (and enacted with an ensemble brilliance that, but for *Drive, He Said,* has probably not been seen in American films since *The Rain People*). Beyond this, *The Godfather* is an incontrovertible demonstration of the continued vitality and artistic power of two things in films whose resources had increasingly been thought to be exhausted: of densely plotted, linear narrative, and of naturalism – social observation and the accumulation of authenticating detail – as a method. And it possesses, moreover, that special excitement and authority available to a film which is both a work of artistic seriousness and one of truly popular appeal, a mass entertainment made without pandering or condescension.

The Godfather is all these things and more, with such immense skill and assurance that I feel almost impatient with my own inability to enjoy it more to escape some nagging dissatisfaction. The basis of that dissatisfaction is perhaps best expressed by the compliment which has been paid to the film by one of its many admirers: that it is the *"Gone with the Wind"* of gangster films. Though *The Godfather* is far better than *Gone with the Wind* one does sometimes feel, as with the earlier film, that the later claims for itself a definitiveness partly on grounds of its being bigger, longer, and more richly upholstered than any other treatment of its subject; the defects of which virtues are such that, compared with *The Godfather,* even a less good film like *The French Connection* can seem to be lighter on its feet. But it is in its attempt at definitiveness in relation to its antecedents in a genre-as a gangster film among other gangster films-that my reservations about *The Godfather* chiefly lie. And despite all the novelty of its variations on familiar material, it is primarily as a genre movie that it has been said, and given my understanding of genres in American movies, is capable of evolution and the absorption of novel variations. Despite which, I am less inclined than is Norman Podhoretz ("Crime & the American Dream," *Commentary,* January 1972) to see that the genre has evolved so far from Robert Warshow's famous exposition of it ("The Gangster as Tragic Hero," in *The Immediate Experience*) as now to present as with unambiguously affirmative images of worldly success. At least I'm far from prepared, as one who has watched (and shared) the responses of an audience as it assents to the killings by the Corleone family in *The Godfather,* to say that the appeal of the gangster in popular art has become one in which sadism no longer plays an important part.

It may be that I speak here from a warped perspective, having devoured in my youth, not biographies of captains of industry, but crime fiction and, fascinated by their chronicles of brutality, Herbert Asbury's trio of informal histories of our urban under-worlds, *The Gangs of New York, The Barbary Coast,* and *The French Quarter.* But what we see of Don Corleone at work is not a man making business deals (except for that running joke of a deal someone cannot refuse – his submission or his life), but, no less than in *Scarface,* a man exercising the nearly limitless power to hurt and intimidate. Even were we given some more detailed pic-ture of what the Corleones's business entailed, it must surely mod-ify our admiration for their success that it involves, if it is not actually based on, killing people; but, fascinating as a depiction of how the family's fortune was acquired and how its businesses are run might be, virtually nothing of the sort is presented (aside from the family's unlikely decision not to become involved in heroin traffic, the effect of which – like that of the family's victims being only other gangsters – is merely to make the Corleones more acceptable to us). Instead, in Robert Warshow's words, "Since we do not see the rational and routine aspects of the gangster's behavior, the practice of brutality – the quality of unmixed crimi-nality – becomes the totality of his career. . . . Thus brutality itself becomes at once the means to success and the content of success – a success that is defined in its most general terms, not as accom-plishment or specific gain, but simply as the unlimited possibility of aggression. (In the same way, film presentations of businessmen tend to make it appear that they achieve their success by talking on the telephone and holding conferences and that success *is* talk-ing on the telephone and holding conferences.)"

The effect of stressing that the Corleones are in business, but limiting our view of their business to the expansion and consoli-dation of their power by their liquidation of the opposition, is to create probably the most consistent depiction of business-as-mur-der since *Monsieur Verdoux. But* despite this, and despite the film's sporadic gestures toward extending its trope of business-as-murder into the political sphere – the allusions to the Kennedys, to Lyn-don Johnson (a meeting of rival mobs commenced with a senti-ment about "reasoning together"), the remark by Michael, Don Corleone's heir, to his fiancee that she is being naive in saying the power of the Corleones is to be distinguished from that of Senators and Presidents because the latter do not kill people – it is not primarily in their aspect of businessmen that we see the gangsters in *The Godfather*. Rather – and one sees here the inadvertent felicity of the notorious expunging of all mention of the word "Mafia" in the film – it is as members of a "family": as godfather, father, grandparent, son, and brother. Though we see Don Corleone occasionally issuing an edict on his business affairs, our predominant images of him are not in his exercise of power but in his domestic role – officiating as father of the bride (in the film's splendid opening sequence), shopping for groceries, playing with his grandchild; not as a Scarface in flashy suits and monogrammed shirts, but as an old man, almost vulnerable-looking in his rumpled clothes and with the trace of gray stubble on his face.

Brando's performance as Don Corleone stands apart from the rest – perhaps inevitably, given all the advance publicity – as a tour de force of mimicry and make-up, but there are few if any other actors whose very presence carries the immense personal authority to be able to play Don Corleone in this peculiarly subdued almost passive way while making credible the sense of his being the architect and administrator of his power. (And despite the sense one has of Brando's power being kept largely under wraps in what is basically a glorified character role, when Don Corleone dies, the absence of Brando in the film is felt as a loss of at least the potential for unleashing his special kind of power). And it is essential to the film's conception of its subject that Don Corleone be played in this way: not as a Verdoux, using his family as the excuse for his zeal in business, but as a man amassing power to provide for his sons and dependents, and finding happiness in the serenity of his garden. If *The Godfather is* most unmistakably of its genre when Don Corleone's regular chauffeur fails to report for work and one knows immediately that an attempt will be made on his employer's life, so the one single thing that most distinguishes *The Godfather* from other gangster films is that Don Corleone is not a doomed overreacher but a man who dies, in effect, in bed.

What is this family whose claims override all others in *The Godfather?* It is, for one thing, a patriarchy, and the story the film has to tell is basically not Don Corleone's but Michael's: a story of his initiation into the family by an act of murder, of the succession of the youngest, most assimilated son to the patriarchal powers and responsibilities and the ethnic mystique of his father. The audience approves Michael's initiation; the narrative thrust of the film is such that it cannot do otherwise; and is made to see the family as to some considerable degree admirable in its colorful ethnicity and fierce loyalties, the strength of its ties that bind. But is *The Godfather* an unambiguous celebration of this family? For a time, while its members are barricaded together from their enemies under the interim reign of Michael's brother, Sonny, there is, even in the sweaty, suffocating togetherness of their confinement, a real sense of *Gemutlichkeit*. But Sonny is a false godfather: hot-headed, bellicose, given to acting impetuously on his feelings without letting the family's interests temper his personal pride; he is, in the classic generic mold, an overreacher, and is killed by what is perhaps the genre's most sustainedly savage hail of machinegun fire. Under Don Corleone and, later, under Michael, what we are aware of instead is a large house whose dark interiors convey no sense of spaciousness, a feudal deference to rank and the lordly granting of dispensations, the suppression of dissent (so as not to give aid and comfort to the family's enemies), and a foundation of blasphemous hypocracy (Michael swearing devotion to God in church while his underlings massacre those who have acted against the family and all others standing in its way). The film's final image is of the new godfather's ring being kissed by a petitioner while a door closes, shutting out Michael's wife to whom, in denying his implication in a killing he had ordered, he has just lied.

Coppola at one time described his work on *The Godfather* as a commercial chore, distinguishable from his direction of a "personal" film like *The Rain People,* and yet, when one thinks back to *The Rain People*'s ambiguous sense of family life as something whose responsibilities, however burdensome, could not be simply left behind, it almost seems that *The Godfather* is a film the director was fated to make, and to make in this way, into a more personal film than he is perhaps aware. But though the degree of emphasis on family life which Coppola brings to *The Godfather* is new to gangster films, the family and familial piety are by no means unknown to the genre (nor – *vide* the Manson "family" – to recent crimes of fact). This is so not only of such late examples as

Bonnie and Clyde and *The Brotherhood*, but of others as early as *The Public Enemy*, in which one already sees a full-blown instance of that sentimentalization of mothers which drifts in and out of the genre and finds its grotesque apotheosis in *White Heat*; and if fathers have generally fared less well as chiefly weak, rebelled-against authority figures, the gangster's mob itself can be seen to be a species of patriarchal family.

What *The Godfather* does is to literalize this similarity: the gang's chieftain is no longer like a patriarch, he is a patriarch; the gang no longer resembles a family but has become one, and not just one more fragmented family among others but virtually the realization of that ideal of the nuclear, fortresslike family with whose images our movies have provided us from the Hardys on up, until, in thrall to newer pieties, they abandoned earlier ones to television. (Thus the importance of situating the Corleones mainly in the 40's as one of the old men in the film says, "Young people don't respect anything these days. Times are changing for the worse.") But is this image of gangsters as the fulfillment and embodiment of our discarded ideals – as the family next door in the 40's – a celebration of the values of which those ideals consist? I think it is rather more like a criticism of them, but a criticism of a peculiarly bland and muffled kind, a criticism to be found less in the content of the film than in the phenomenon of our response to it: in our ability to accept gangsters as embodiments of such values. *Within* the film, the ambiguity of its celebration of family life is never violated: thus the rightness of Brando's decision, reportedly on his own initiative, to refuse to speak (to the Corleones's lawyer) the line, "A man with a briefcase can steal more than a hundred men with guns"; any such betrayal of conscious cynicism would be fatally to tip the scales in which the film is so precariously balanced. But the effect of domesticating the genre in this way is less to subject familial values to a criticism than to strip the gangster of his mythic dimension and his tragic meaning for us: to convert him into only one more of those "good husbands and fathers" so familiar to us from the crimes of bureaucrats and obedient soldiers. The gangster has here ceased to be, in Warshow's words, "what we want to be and what we are afraid we may become," and has become instead only another instance of the banality of evil. Who is this good husband and father, this man who must occasionally kill people in order to provide? He is only a man not unlike us, who has gone, perhaps, a little too far; and if our families are less the invincible fortress than is his, we have at least the comfort of knowing that our crimes are small in comparison; we can, with equanimity, cultivate our gardens. But at its best – whether in a *Scarface's* conceit of the Capone mob as the Borgias in Chicago or a *Quick Millions's* sardonic version of capitalist enterprise or a *White Heat's* vision of the gangster as a wife-nagged, mother-fixated, "tension-head-ache"-wracked, upwardly-mobile striver-the effect of the gangster genre was to press us to recognition of the source in us of the gangster's disturbing hold on our imaginations. What are we that in this outsize, driven figure and his terrible excesses we can see the image, however extravagant and distorted, of ourselves?

THE TWO GODFATHERS

DAVID DENBY

"The Two Godfathers" first appeared in *Partisan Review*, vol. 43, no. 1, 1976.

Near the end of her review of *The Godfather* (Part One), Pauline Kael wrote, "These gangsters *like* their life style, while we – seeing it from outside – are appalled," and, Kael concluded, "Nothing is resolved at the end of *The Godfather*, because the family business goes on. Terry Malloy didn't clean up the docks at the end of *On the Waterfront;* that was a lie. *The Godfather* is popular melodrama, but it expresses a new tragic realism." It's often hard to tell who's included in Kael's "we" (on any given occasion she may mean the entire movie audience, the readers of *The New Yorker*, or a limited group of like-minded persons), but if she intended to characterize the likely common response, she was way of the mark. Most people obviously were not appalled by the gangsters, and I doubt that many viewed the continuation of the Corleone enterprise or any other element in the movie as tragic. For all its pessimism and violence, *The Godfather* was hugely enjoyed as a kind of grisly comedy. These mad, paradoxical killers – sadistic and pious, flamboyant and self-abasing – awed and amused the audience with the weirdly archaic style of their behavior. Feudatories in the corporate age, dour celebrants of obscure codes and implacable loyalties, they killed with such fervent sensuality they were almost romantic.

At the same time, they were no threat to us. Mario Puzo and Francis Ford Coppola were very shrewd about this, and more than a little disingenuous. They knew the public loathes ordinary, unorganized movie criminals – muggers and rapists and rooftop singers – and regularly applauds when Clint Eastwood wipes them out like vermin. Thus in their movie about the aristocrats of crime they were careful never to suggest that the audience itself could be hurt by any of these fellows; indeed, all the everyday victims of Mafia extortion and violence (store-owners, truckers, union members, etc.) were simply omitted, and the issue of harm to society at large was never raised, leaving us (meaning nearly everyone) free to enjoy the intramural mayhem without anxiety. Since Puzo and Coppola did no more than barely outline the economic causes of Mafia rivalry, conducting endless, incomprehensible vendettas seemed to be the gangsters' sole activity, the sole definition of what a gangster was. Odd, often very funny, but certainly not tragic.

I don't mean to imply that Puzo and Coppola let us off the hook entirely. The Corleones might have been merely exotic, irrelevant to America's central concerns, but in a twist to the joke, Puzo and Coppola patterned their Mafia types after American big businessmen at the turn of the century – those grim Horatio Algers, predatory heroes in the war of all against all. In *The Godfather*, as opposed to the Kefauver hearings, the Mafia was not simply some imported ideology or conspiracy; it was the result of two cultures meeting and interlocking, the grafting of one tradition of fraud and violence (Sicilian) onto another (American). I believe the audience, far from being appalled, widely accepted this cool "sociological" or "historical" view of the Corleones – that they were immigrants pursuing a corrupt but distinctly American road to power and status because legitimate roads had been closed to them – and also accepted and admired their success. The brilliant triumph of the movie itself, its glittering power as a media event, only confirmed that the Mafia had made it – at least in terms of public appreciation. The explosive question of whether the public's use of the words "Mafia" and "Cosa Nostra" constituted an insult to Italian-Americans faded as an issue once *The Godfather* had become such an irresistible success, for in this country the large-scale media exposure of a given phenomenon often creates legitimacy-through-celebrity. In no time at all, a widely publicized "spur" can become, if not a badge of pride, then at least a means of plugging into the irresistible circuits of media excitement – in other words, an advantage. "It makes me proud to be an Italian," a man behind me said to his companions at the end of the movie, and he said it without irony.

Perhaps he was proud (and non-Italians admiring) because, in the movie's central conceit, the Corleones were that rare thing in America, a happy family; and they were portrayed – at least in the first half of the movie – as a model of health, yes, as happy monsters whose violent behavior emerged from a high appetite for life as much as from the family's peculiar way of doing business. The ambivalence was morally audacious for a popular movie, and it's a mark of Coppola's skill that he got almost everyone to accept it. By the time Michael Corleone shoots his father's enemies in the restaurant scene, Coppola had most of us where he wanted us; the hair-raising use of conventional narrative techniques secured our acquiescence and complicity. With an awed laugh, directed at ourselves as much as the screen, we accepted the notion that Michael's violence was an act of family piety, a way of accepting his father, his family past, his natural destiny.

Those few who didn't accept it, who were alarmed by the mixture of graciousness and murder, complained of sentimentality. For the anti-sentimentalists there was too much happiness in the Corleone family and too much pictorial beauty in the movie. Despite the disingenuous strategy of *The Godfather* that I mentioned earlier, the charge of sentimentality makes no sense to me. It ignores the entire second half of the movie, where Michael Corleone gradually becomes an isolated and ruthless killer, up to the remarkable moment when he looks his wife straight in the eye and lies, shutting her out forever. As for the ingratiating visual quality of the film, a grainy, intentionally sordid photographic style would actually have been the more conventional option for a gangster movie. Instead, Coppola emphasized the beauty of the gangsters' lives in both Sicily and America, increasing our sense of moral squalor and violation: they lived in beauty and acted vilely. In any case, it's a great natural advantage for a movie to be physically beautiful if the director and cinematographer know what they're doing, and Francis Ford Coppola and Gordon Willis's work was hardly the soft-focus lyricism of commercial hacks. During the shimmering, slightly overexposed Sicilian sequences we are meant to feel the corruption gathering in the lemon and green ripeness of the countryside. Sicily, that eternally fouled paradise! The rottenness became an emanation of its heat and sun. This may not impress historians or political scientists very much, but it's the most expressive kind of movie shorthand. The dark brown and red American interiors, a setting for secrets and plots, carried associations of the corrupted stained-leather atmosphere, the phony distinguished style, of boardrooms, manor libraries, and clubs. Like so much of the best popular art, *The Godfather* was almost seductively easy and pleasurable, but its pleasurableness functioned for the audience as a variety of knowledge – we were provoked by the satisfaction the movie gave us into new forms of understanding.

The *Godfather II* is also extraordinarily beautiful, but it's a much slower, heavier, more obviously ironic film, without the paralyzing energy, audacious wit, or imperious command of the audience. Admirers have found a quality of new "depth," but to me it feels like new weight. On the other hand, cynics who assume the film was made simply to sustain an earlier box-office triumph are dead wrong – this one wasn't made only for the money. My complaint is that it draws on Part One with rather dismaying reverence and over-explicitness, dulling the interest – through sheer attenuation – of ideas that were clear and forceful in the earlier film's closing scenes: the increasing isolation of the Americanized Mafioso, Michael Corleone, and the persistence of Sicilian patterns of "honor" through the generations. In Part One the cultural mix of Sicily and America produced some episodes that were funny and bizarrely "right" (the men plotting tribal vengeance over a take-home dinner) and also a convincing denouement. In Part Two, however, the intercutting of America in the sixties with earlier periods in Sicily and Little Italy produces the effect of a pattern sustained by will power and heavy labor after its logic has collapsed. Now that Michael's so completely an American it's no

longer unequivocally "right" that he act with Sicilian thorough-
ness and cruelty at the end, murdering his own brother. At least
the act requires some further explanation, but Puzo and Coppola
have allowed their "pattern" to assume the work that should be
done in a narrative film by old-fashioned motivation. The results
are hollow, mechanical on a grand scale, and incomprehensible.
They try to place the "sociological" view of Italian-American crime
in historical perspective, ranging from Fanucci, the florid turn-of-
the-century neighborhood extortionist in white suite and erotic
moustaches, to Michael Corleone, grey-suited, corporate-cold,
ruthlessly presiding over the fouling of contemporary America
with WASP and Jew as equal partner. This is beguiling as social history but extremely vague as information on the details of criminal
activity in any period. After six hours and twenty minutes of film I
still haven't understood how a single one of these gangsters actually operates.

What is it about the theme of immigration to the United States
that brings out the reverent worst in writers, directors, critics?
Oscar Handlin's famous book, *The Uprooted,* was so heavily stuffed
with large, noble emotions and heroic travail, and so lacking in
individual experience and feelings that I couldn't get through it.
In the same vein, Jan Troell's epic film, *The Emigrants,* leads onto
the suffering shoulders of its hero and heroine every typical problem of leavetaking, oceanic crossing, and settlement in the new
land without ever creating much interest in either of them as
characters. Coppola, too, depends on the universal, the typical,
the general whenever he comes in sight of the Statue of Liberty.
He shoots young Vito's entrance into New York harbor and passage through customs and Ellis Island as a blandly monumental
picture-essay in *Life*-magazine style; his Little Italy movie-street is
so packed with bustling-immigrant-life cliches that, except for a
scene in a working-class theater and another in front of a Punch
and Judy show, one's eye never takes in anything in particular.
Apparently, mere individuality would be too small, too eccentric,
and mean-spirited individuality practically an outrage against the
immigration theme's familiar ideal of suffering virtue. When Vito
grows up into a gallant neighborhood protector, an urban Robin
Hood, he's almost totally unreal – a dreamboat immigrant-gang-
ster. Suffused in creamy, glamorous light (banal as an Italian

"chromo" in the scenes with mother and child), Robert De Niro establishes the physical antecedents of the Brando character (soft, cracked voice and emotional reserve) but not the viciousness, the physical menace of the future extortionist, murderer, and big-time gangster. In these scenes the "sociological" view of crime has been used as a way of softening the criminal.

A movie epic needs an eccentric character as its focus or else it solemnly tells us what we already know. Unfortunately, as Michael Corleone grows older he becomes another of those familiar, semi-mythological American bastards, an obscenely rich and completely lonely man of great power. This is no surprise and not terribly interesting. The notion that extreme success in America isolates you from everything worth striving for is now too complacent and banal an *apercu* to sustain the grandiose and solemn treatment it gets here. If Puzo and Coppola aren't going to turn Michael into an entertaining grotesque, couldn't they develop him, open him up a bit? Poor Al Pacino, locked in an unyielding, inarticulate funk, stares and stares and becomes a bore – of baffling intensity, but a bore nonetheless. The final scenes, with Michael brooding over his darkened blue lake while memories of the family he's decimated torture his mind, resound with the hollow certainty of an irony too easily achieved. In Part One Coppola escaped from those moralists who wanted the Corleones to be *unhappy,* but now he's succumbed.

Still, despite all one's dissatisfactions, Coppola appears to be a uniquely central and powerful American talent. His feeling for American surfaces – the glancing intimations of social status is gesture, tone of voice, decor, clothes – is as precise as any director's in American film history. Perhaps one has to cite John O'Hara for the proper comparison, but Coppola is more playful. His showpiece big party scene near the beginning of Part Two, an obvious contrast with Part One's wedding celebration, depends on observation so acute it becomes a form of malicious wit. The Corleones have charged into the American center by the late fifties, and they've paid the price in blandness: their lakeside bash is a ceremonial drag, more like a TV variety show than a party; the hearty Italian street music has been replaced by a suave-sounding dance band and a blond cherub's chorus, the natural gaiety by a desperate desire to have fun. Having moved the base of their operations from Long Island to Lake Tahoe, they've fallen in with Western WASPs, or at least the dissolute remainders of a WASP ruling class – a pious, hollow-voiced senator (played by G. D. Spradlin as a degenerate combination of Edward Gurney and Ed Sullivan) and blond playmates for brother Fredo and sister Connie (Connie's lover, in a cruelly symbolic casting stroke, is acted by the washed-up juvenile Troy Donahue). Coppola rarely emphasizes this sort of thing; he depends on our memories, our powers of observation, and our willingness to make connections without having them spelled out. When Michael visits Hyman Roth, the millionaire Jewish gangster with the middle-class family life style, the hilarious mediocrity of Roth's Miami home – pale yellow walls and wicker furniture, darkened little TV room, recessive wife serving lunch on a portable table – is so eloquently expressive of the habitual practice of fraud that one is convinced that realism is not only the most natural but the most magical of cinematic modes.

Coppola's unusual curiosity about such things as fatherhood, marriage, power, spiritual anguish, etc., sets him apart from the run of Hollywood directors as a central interpreter of American experience, a man taking the big risks, working outside the limits of traditional genres. The lack of eccentricity or repeating obsession, the avoidance of obvious visual metaphor or radical foreshortening of narrative may deceive some viewers into declaring there's no artist behind the perfectly achieved images, the marvelous amplitude and evenness of flow, but that would be a mistake induced by the influence of the auteur theory on educated taste. Those looking for "personality" – the flourishes of "signature" – may be too distracted to feel the power of Coppola's work. His personality (sad word) emerges in the way he chooses to reveal his characters. For instance, he has a genius for noisy, shallow, self-propelling types – the American as untrammeled egotist, powerful and infantile at the same time. He appears to love their theatrical energy and flash, and his sense of how such people behave in social situations is so accurate that he can do very funny scenes without a trace of caricature. He's at his best in the convention of "surveillance experts" in *The Conversation*. Boastful, frenetic, absurdly aggressive, these American go-getters can't stop competing for a moment, not even at a party, and so they begin showing off their skills and playing dirty tricks on one another. Their casual cruelty while "relaxing," their amiable, thoughtless dedication to "professionalism" as a biding justification for any act, gradually produces a kind of horror that is all the more powerful for coming at us so obliquely. The sequence never ceases to play at its quiet, evenly sustained level of observation, yet the reverberations are tragic; it's hard not to think of soldiers testing weapons in Vietnam and other recent examples of American professionals run amuck. To expose the murderous falsity of appearances without betraying the appearances themselves remains one of the principal tasks of realism and one of the things movies do most successfully. Coppola's work, at its best, sustains the highest traditions of realism. Despite everything that can be marked off against him, there's every reason to expect Coppola to be a principal exponent of American themes in the movies of the next two decades.

INTERVIEW: FRANCIS FORD COPPOLA, *PLAYBOY,* JULY 1975.

WILLIAM MURRY

Excerpts from interview reprinted by courtesy of *Playboy.*

PLAYBOY: One of the most important areas you explore in *Godfather II* is the connection between Mafia operations and some of our legitimate big-business interests. Are you saying that some corporations are no better and no worse than organized crime?

COPPOLA: Right from the very beginning it became clear, as I was doing my research, that though the Mafia was a Sicilian phenomenon, there was no way it could really have flowered except in the soil of America. America was absolute ripe for the Mafia. Everything the Mafia believed in and was set up to handle – absolute control, the carving out of territories, the rigging of prices and the elimination of competition – everything was here. In fact, the corporate philosophy that built some of our biggest industries and great personal fortunes was a Mafia philosophy. So when those Italians arrived here, they found themselves in the perfect place.

It became clear to me that there was a wonderful parallel to be drawn, that the career of Michael Corleone was the perfect metaphor for the new land. Like America, Michael began as a clean, brilliant young man endowed with incredible resources and believing in a humanistic idealism. Like America, Michael was the child of an older system, a child of Europe. Like America, Michael was an innocent who had tried to correct the ills and injustices of his progenitors. But then he got blood on his hands. He lied to himself and to others about what he was doing and why. And so he became not only the mirror image of what he'd come from but worse. One of the reasons I wanted to make *Godfather II* is that I wanted to take Michael to what I felt was the logical conclusion. He wins every battle; his brilliance and his resources enable him to defeat all his enemies. I didn't want Michael to die. I didn't want Michael to be put into prison. I didn't want him to be assassinated by his rivals. But, in a bigger sense, I also wanted to destroy Michael. There's no doubt that, by the end of this picture, Michael Corleone, having beaten everyone, is sitting there alone, a living corpse.

PLAYBOY: Is that your metaphor for America today?

COPPOLA: Unlike America, Michael Corleone is doomed. There's no way that man is ever going to change. I admit I considered some upbeat touch at the end, like having his son turn against him to indicate he wouldn't follow in that tradition, but honesty – and Pacino – wouldn't let me do it. Michael is doomed. But I don't at all feel that America is doomed. I thought it was healthy to make this horror-story statement – as a warning, if you like – but, as a nation, we don't have to go down that same road, and I don't think we will.

PLAYBOY: A number of critics feel that you and others – including, perhaps, *Playboy*, with its series on organized crime – helped romanticize the Mafia in America. How do you respond to that?

COPPOLA: Well, first of all, the Mafia was romanticized in the book. And I was filming that book. To do a film about my real opinion of the Mafia would be another thing altogether. But it's a mistake to think I was making a film about the Mafia. *Godfather Part I* is a romance about a king with three sons. It is a film about power. It could have been the Kennedys. The whole idea of a family living in a compound – that was all based on Hyannisport. Remember, it wasn't a documentary about Mafia chief Vito Genovese. It was Marlon Brando with Kleenex in his mouth.

Select Bibliography

SELECT BIBLIOGRAPHY

Ambrogio, Anthony. "'The Godfather, I and II': Patterns of Corruption," *Film Criticism* 3(1), Fall 1978, 35–44.
Chown, Jeffrey. *Hollywood Auteur: Francis Coppola*. New York: Praeger Publishers, 1988.
Cowie, Peter. *Coppola: A Biography*, updated ed. New York: Da Capo Press, 1994.
The Godfather Book. London: Faber & Faber, 1997.
Evans, Robert. *The Kid Stays in the Picture*. New York: Hyperion, 1994.
Goodwin, Michael, and Naomi Wise. *On the Edge: The Life and Times of Francis Coppola*. New York: William Morrow & Company, 1989.
Johnson, Robert. *Francis Ford Coppola*. Boston: Twayne Publishers, 1977.
Lebo, Harlan. *The Godfather Legacy*. New York: Simon & Schuster, 1997.
Lewis, Jon. *Whom God Wishes to Destroy: Francis Coppola and the New Hollywood*. Durham, NC: Duke University Press, 1995.
Kolker, Robert. *The Cinema of Loneliness*. New York: Oxford University Press, 1980.
Macksey, Richard. "'The Glitter of the Infernal Stream': The Splendors and Miseries of Francis Coppola." *Bennington Review* 15, 1983, 2–16.
Puzo, Mario. *The Godfather*. New York: G. P. Putnam's Sons, 1969.
The Godfather Papers and Other Confessions. New York: G. P. Putnam's Sons, 1972.
Shadoian, Jack. *Dreams and Dead Ends: The American Gangster/Crime Film*. Cambridge, MA and London, Eng.: The MIT Press, 1977.
Zuker, Joel S. *Francis Ford Coppola: A Guide to References and Resources*. Boston: G. K. Hall & Company, 1984.

Index

1900, 151, 152

Airport, 23, 35
Al Capone, 81, 112
Altabello, Don, 9–10
American Graffiti, 39
American Zoetrope, *see* Zoetrope
Andolini, Donna, 91
Angels with Dirty Faces, 111
Apocalypse Now, 11, 12, 38–9, 43
Assante, Armand, 71
Aubrey, James, 28
Auden, W.H., 134, 142
Auteur movies, 29–30, 36, 37
Avakian, Aram, 30

Baby Face Nelson, 112
"Baccagghiu," 72
Barrow, Clyde, 112–3
Bart, Peter, 26–7, 30, 51
Barthes, Roland, 106 n.4
Barzini (godfather), 6, 114–5
Batman, 47
Behind the Green Door, 39
Bells of St. Mary's, The, 128–30
Bertolucci, Bernardo, 39, 133
Big Sleep, The, 81
Bluhdorn, Charles, 24, 40, 44–5, 51

Bob, Carol, Ted and Alice, 23
Bogart, Humphrey, 111
Bonasera (character), 115, 116
Bonnie and Clyde, 14, 110, 112–3, 127
Bonnie Parker Story, The, 112
Bram Stoker's Dracula, 13
Brando, Marlon, 3, 28–9, 41, 53 n.20; n.29
Brasi, Luca, 6, 115
Bronx Story, A, 112
Brotherhood, The, 26, 81
Brusca, Giovanni, 73
Bullets or Ballots, 111
Buscetta, Tommaso, 62–3

Caan, James, 28
Cabaret, 36
Cagney, James, 81, 110, 111
Camonte, Tony, 83–5, 89
Capitalism
  gangster films and, 110, 113
  in *Godfather II*, 86–7, 118, 120–2
  in *Godfather* trilogy, 113, 152–3
  Mafia and, 120
Capone, Al, 81, 83, 84, 106 n.20, 111
Carlito's Way, 112
Carlo (Connie's husband), 6, 7

Carridi, Carmine, 28
Cavalleria Rusticana (opera),
    140–3
    Godfather III and, 10, 133,
    145–6
Chinatown, 127
Church
    in Cavalleria Rusticana, 142–3
    in Godfather trilogy, 14, 16,
    143, 145
    Mafia and, 59
Clarens, Carlos, 65, 69, 106 n.20
Clement, Catherine, 148–9, 154
Clemenza (character), 7, 92
Clockwork Orange, A, 36
Codes of honor, 89–90, 140–1
    in Godfather III, 103–4
    law vs., 94
Coming to America, 45
Community standards, 40
Comolli, Louis, 128
Conversation, The, 11, 12, 38, 43
Coppola, Carmine, 80
Coppola, Francis Ford
    aesthetic of films, 2–3
    biography, 10–3
    cinematic style, 3–4
    debts, 50, 56 n.65
    on Godfather trilogy, 4
    opera and, 133–4
    pay for Godfather II, 41
    pay for Godfather III, 47–8
    and production of Godfather II,
    40–43
    and production of Godfather III,
    47–52
    and production of The
    Godfather, 26–32
Coppola, Gio, 103
Coppola, Sofia, 48, 102–3
Corleone, Anthony, 7, 9, 119,
    125, 146

Corleone, Appolonia, 91
Corleone, Connie, 5, 8, 9, 91,
    119, 120, 125
Corleone, Fredo, 6, 8, 120, 122,
    150
Corleone, Kay, 6, 7, 8, 68–9, 91,
    119, 146
Corleone, Mama, 90, 91
Corleone, Mary, 9, 10, 102, 103,
    126, 133, 145–6
Corleone, Michael, 6–10, 15
    in baptism sequence, 117, 144,
    150
    capitalism and, 96–7
    confession, 150–1
    death, 103
    decline, 150–1
    deromanticization of, 118–20
    isolation of, 126
    Italian investments, 100
    Mafia ethics and, 65–6
    paralleled with Vito, 122–3, 126
    personal vs. professional, 121–3
    redemption, 102, 125–6
    relationship with Kay, 68–9,
    117
    in Sicily, 141
    as southern Italian male, 89–90
    struggle for legitimacy, 66
    wealth and power, 101–2
Corleone, Sonny, 6, 89, 115
Corleone, Vito
    assassination attempt on, 6,
    129–30
    death, 6, 103
    family life, 121
    goes to theatre, 87
    immigration, 122, 153
    murder of Fanucci, 87–8, 90,
    100, 143–4
    paralleled with Michael, 122–3,
    126

as southern Italian male, 89–90
    in wedding sequence, 5–6,
    116–7
Corleone family
    as "aristocracy," 99, 101–2
    decline of, 86, 138
    deromanticization of, 118, 120
    mainstreaming of, 120–1,
        123–4, 152–3
    romanticization of, 116–7
Cotton Club, The, 29
Cowie, Peter, 25, 31
Crime genre, 13–4, 15–6, *see also*
    Gangster films
    women in, 67–8
Crocodile Dundee, 45

Daisy Miller, 38
Damned, The, 151
Damone, Vic, 33
Davis, Martin, 44, 46–7
Deep Throat, 39
Dementia 13, 11
De Niro, Robert, 112
Depression, Great, 112
Devil and Miss Jones, The, 39
Diamonds Are Forever, 36
Diller, Barry, 40, 42, 44–5, 55–6
    n.65–6
Director's Company, 36–9
Dirty Harry, 36
Duvall, Robert, 48

"E" category films, 128
Eisner, Michael, 45
Evans, Robert, 24–32, 40–1, 53
    n.28, 79
Exorcist, The, 38

Falcone, Giovanni, 73
Family
    in *Godfather* trilogy, 14–5, 60

Fanucci, Don, 87–8, 90, 100,
    143–4
Farber, Stephen, 131 n.6
Fatal Attraction, 45
FBI Story, The, 112
Fiddler on the Roof, 36
Five Easy Pieces, 127
Fontaine, Johnny, 115, 116
Friedkin, William, 38

Gambino, Carlo, 71
Gangster films, *see also* Crime
    genre
    authenticity of, 80–2
    ideology of, 109–14
Gangsters
    hubris of, 110–2
    law and, 14
Gang That Couldn't Shoot Straight,
    The, 28
Geary, Senator, 8, 119
Gilday, Archbishop, 124
G-Men, 111
Godfather
Godfather, The
    Academy Awards and, 1–2, 35,
        54 n.3
    authenticity of, 78–82
    baptism sequence, 7, 65, 117,
        144
    capitalism and, 114
    cinematography, 93
    earnings of, 34–5, 36
    editing of, 30
    family and, 78, 115, 116–7
    as fantasy, 95–7
    ideology in, 114–7
    Italian Americans in, 82–3, 86,
        88–92
    Mafia and, 57, 65–8, 88, 117
    music, 91, 136–7
    narrative, 2–3

Godfather, The (continued)
  nostalgia in, 92–4, 96
  opening sequence, 4, 86
  pastness in, 93
  premiere, 34
  production, 25–35
  Scarface and, 82–5
  Sicily in, 91–2
  submerged ethnicity in, 94–7
  synopsis, 5–7
  wedding scene, 5, 114–7,
    136–7, 138
  women in, 90–1
Godfather II
  Academy Awards and, 1–2,
    42–3
  capitalism and, 86–7, 118,
    120–2
  deromanticization in, 119–22
  family in, 86, 118–23
  First Communion sequence, 7,
    119, 138–9
  ideology in, 118–23
  murder of Fanucci sequence,
    143–4
  narrative, 3
  parallel structure, 122–3
  production, 35–43
  synopsis, 7–8
Godfather III, 97–105
  Academy Awards and, 49
  codes of honor in, 103–4
  cost, 47–8, 48–9
  death of Mary Corleone
    sequence, 145–6
  earnings, 49
  editing of, 48
  family in, 99, 124–6
  father/daughter drama, 146–51
  humor in, 101–2
  ideology in, 123–7
  Italian festa sequence, 100–1

Italy in, 99–100, 101–2
  nostalgia in, 153–4
  production, 43–52
  rights for, 49
  salaries paid, 47–8
  Scarface and, 101
  submerged ethnicity in, 104
  synopsis, 8–10
  visual world, 98
Godfather trilogy
  The Bells of St. Mary's and,
    128–30
  capitalism in, 60, 113
  Church in, 14, 16, 143, 145
  color in, 69, 98
  dialogue in, 3–4
  family and, 14–5, 60, 138–9
  Francis Ford Coppola on, 4
  Italian Americans in, 105
  law in, 14, 16
  light in, 69
  as metaphor for capitalism,
    60
  national history and, 151–4
  opera and, 135–6
  as progressive film, 127–30
  sexual relationships in, 68–9
  social world, 14–5
  writing on, 4
Gold Diggers of 1933, The, 113
Goodbye Columbus, 32
Gotti, John, 71
Graduate, The, 127
Gramsci, Antonio, 154–5 n.1
Gulf & Western, 23–4, 35, 37,
    45–6

Hagen, Tom, 6, 115, 122
Hamilton, George, 48
Harvey, Anthony, 31
Hays Code, 65, 81, 111
Hello Dolly, 23

Hess, John, 86
Hollywood General Studios, 12
Hugo, Victor, 147

Immobiliare, *see* Societa General
    Immobiliare
Individualism, 97, 109–10
Italian-American Civil Rights
    League, 32, 33
Italian Americans
    in *The Godfather*, 82–3, 85–6,
        88–92
    in *Godfather III*, 99–105
    in *Godfather* trilogy, 105
    organized crime and, 76–7, 82
    in *Scarface*, 83–5
Italy
    attitude toward Mafia, 64, 73
    in *Godfather III*, 99–100, 101–2

Jaffe, Stanley, 24
Jameson, Fredric, 77–8, 92–3,
    114, 123–4, 131 n.4
John Paul I, Pope, 51, 124

Kael, Pauline, 42
Kazan, Elia, 31, 53 n.29
Keaton, Diane, 48
Kerkorian, Kirk, 28
Kerman, Joseph, 135–6
Key Largo, 81, 111
King, Morgana, 90
Kiss of Death, 111
Klinger, Barbara, 128
Konchalovski, Andrei, 44
Korshak, Sidney, 28

Lamberto, Cardinal, 10, 125
Lancaster, Burt, 26
Last Emperor, The, 151
Last Picture Show, 36
Last Tango in Paris, 39

Law
    code of honor *vs.*, 94
    gangsters and, 14, 94, 111
    in *Godfather* trilogy, 14, 16, 94
Lenny, 127
Leopard, The, 151–2
Lichtenstein, Grace, 32
Little Big Man, 25
Little Caesar, 80, 110, 111
Love Story, 25, 35
Lucas, George, 11, 27
Lucchesi (Vatican official), 9–10

Machine Gun Kelly, 112
Madonna, 48
Mafia
    ambiguity, 58–9
    betrayal and, 62–3
    capitalism and, 60, 120, 124
    Church and, 59
    code, 57, 71–2
    double morality, 59–60
    family and, 60
    in *The Godfather*, 65–8, 88, 117
    incarceration and, 62
    Italian mentality and, 59
    mainstreaming, 70–1, 123–4
    the media and, 73–4
    as metaphor for America, 118
    mythology, 57–64
    origin of name, 58
    in popular culture, 64–5
    poverty and, 62
    regional identity, 66
    secrecy, 72
    sexual roles in, 67–8
    socioeconomics, 60–1
    women and, 67–8
Mafioso, 57, 58, 64
Mancini, Vincent, 9, 10, 101, 126
Mancuso, Frank, 44, 45, 47–8, 49
Marchi, John, 33

Mash, 23
Mature, Victor, 111
May, Elaine, 31
MCA, 46
McCabe and Mrs. Miller, 127
McCluskey (police captain), 6, 116
Media, the
    influence on Mafia, 73–4
    violence in, 74
Milius, John, 38–9
Mitchell, John, 32, 33–4
Muni, Paul, 110
Murphy, Eddie, 44, 45

Narboni, Jean, 128
Nashville, 128
Ness, Elliot, 111–2
Nostalgia films, 92–3

O'Brien, Pat, 111
Ola, Johnny, 120
One from the Heart, 12–3, 43, 50,
    56 n.65
Opera
    in *Godfather* trilogy, 133–54
    movies and, 133–6

Pacino, Al, 3, 28, 41–2, 48, 112
Paper Moon, 38
Paramount Studios, 23–4, 34–5,
    44–6, 52 n.8, 55 n.53
Parker, Bonnie, 112–3
Patton, 11, 23
Peggy Sue Got Married, 13
Penn, Arthur, 31
Pennino, Francesco, 87
Pentangeli, Frankie, 7, 8, 92, 119,
    120
Photography, 153–4
La Piovra (TV series), 64
Poizat, Michel, 134
Poseidon Adventure, The, 39

Pretty Boy Floyd, 112
Production Code, *see* Hays Code
Public Enemy, 81, 110, 111
Pulp Fiction, 75
Puzo, Mario, 25, 32, 66, 73,
    79–80

Radical films, 127–8
Rain People, The, 11
Rigoletto (opera), 146–9
Riina, Toto, 62–3
Rise and Fall of Legs Diamond, The,
    112
Roaring Twenties, The, 111
Robinson, Edward G., 110, 111
Ross, Steve, 47
Rosato brothers, 7, 120
Roth, Hyman, 7, 119, 120
Ruddy, Al, 32, 33–4, 80
Rumble Fish, 13
Ryder, Winona, 48

Scarface, 80–1, 82–5, 93–4, 101,
    110
Schatz, Thomas, 111
Security Pacific Bank, 50
Senso, 134
Sicily, 140–1
    in *The Godfather,* 91–2
    social class in, 61
Sindona, Michele, 51–2
Singer, Jack, 50
Social order, gangster films and,
    111–3
Societa General Immobiliare, 9,
    51
Sollozzo ("the Turk"), 6, 116
Spider's Strategem, The, 134
St. Valentine's Day Massacre, The,*
    81
Stallone, Sylvestor, 44
Stella, Frank, 76

Taxi Driver, 128
Three Men and a Baby, 45
THX-1138, 11
Tomassino, Don, 9
Top Gun, 45
La Traviata (opera), 149
Travolta, John, 43
Tribune Corporation, 46
Tucker: The Man and His Dream,
  13, 44, 56 n.65

Untouchables, The, 111–2

Vatican, the, 9, 145
Verdi, Giuseppe, 148–9, 154–5
  n.1
Verga, Giovanni, 140
"Verismo," 142
Viacom, 46
"La Via Vecchia," 88, 89, 90, 92,
  103
Violence
  the media and, 74

in movies, 14, 15–6
Visconti, Luchino, 133–4

Warner Brothers, 26–7, 80
Warner Communications (WCI),
  46
What's Up Doc?, 36
Wieser, George, 25–6
Willis, Gordon, 93
Women
  in crime genre, 67–8
  in *The Godfather,* 90–1
  Mafia and, 67–8
Woodstock, 23

X-rated films, 39–40

Yablans, Frank, 24, 35, 36–8, 39,
  40, 41, 42

Zaza, Joey, 9, 101
Zinner, Peter, 30
Zoetrope, 11, 12–3, 26